So You Want to Write about American Indians?

So You Want to Write about American Indians?

A Guide for Writers, Students, and Scholars

Devon Abbott Mihesuah

University of Nebraska Press

Lincoln and London

© 2005 by Devon Abbott Mihesuah
All rights reserved. Manufactured in
the United States of America
Set in Adobe Minion by Bob Reitz.
Book designed by Richard Eckersley.
Printed by Edwards Brothers, Inc.
 ∞
Library of Congress Cataloging-in-
Publication Data
Mihesuah, Devon A. (Devon Abbott)
So you want to write about American
Indians?: a guide for writers, students,
and scholars / Devon Abbott
Mihesuah.
p. cm.
Includes bibliographical references
and index.
ISBN 0-8032-8298-2 (pbk.: alk. paper)
1. Authorship. 2. Indians of North
America – Research – Methodology.
I. Title.
PN146.M54 2005   808'.06697—dc22
2004020659

To Uncle Dawson and Aunt Betty Watson

Contents

Preface

So you want to write about American Indians. Tens of thousands of books and essays about Indigenous people are already on the library shelves, and at the rate they are being published it appears that many more are on the way. That's a lot of writing, but surprisingly all this investigation and imagining has only scratched the surface of the complexity of Native America. Perhaps your thesis, dissertation, book, novel, or essay will be unique and will assist in educating America about how tribes lived – and still live – and can offer solutions to the myriad problems tribes face.

This is not a book that offers detailed instructions about grammar, plot development, or writing mysteries. Many readers already know how to find information in libraries, how to outline essays and books, and how the publication process works. These readers may find some of the information here similar to what they have learned from basic English courses and from their own publication experiences. Others are familiar with how to approach tribes for permission to write about them and how to conduct interviews.

Still, I am consistently asked questions about how to write, where to find ideas, how to submit a proposal to tribes, and how to submit essays and book manuscripts to journal editors and book publishers. Even writers with many published books and essays are curious about how others find and organize data. I certainly am. Many more are frustrated by the processes of submitting their work and peer review, and they want to know how they can make their experiences smoother. Therefore, I have tried to incorporate the most common questions and concerns that I repeatedly hear regarding writing and publishing about American Indians. Some readers will notice that I have missed a few aspects of the business, but I hope all readers will find some useful tips.

This book contains a chapter on writing fiction. The field of American Indian literary criticism has exploded, and today there are hundreds of Natives and non-Natives writing poetry, novels, and short stories. While some of this work might be considered "popular" writing – that is, the work is geared toward mainstream America and not toward Natives or academics – the process of gathering ideas, finding inspiration, and locating publishers is similar to what nonfiction writers face. Many Native writers (such as Elizabeth Cook-Lynn, Paula Gunn Allen, Daniel Justice, Craig Womack, Gerald Vizenor, and Jack Forbes) are interested in writing both fiction and nonfiction, and their academic and "mainstream" work are inexorably tied together. The most prevalent readers of Native literature are scholars in the academy who make it their business to dissect and analyze what fellow Native writers have to say.

This book is as a primer for those contemplating writing about Natives and for those who have already experienced writing success. It offers ideas for research, inspiration, and organization. Also included are discussions of key concepts that every author writing about Natives should be aware of: stereotypes, author bias, the politics of publishing, ethics in research and writing, accountability in research and language use, ethnic fraud, and contract negotiation. This book is for students and established writers, for those who have completed an essay or book and do not know how to find a publisher, and for those who cannot figure out why they are unable to find a publisher for their work.

I don't consider myself to be a particularly good writer, but I am persistent. I have never taken a literature class or a course on creative writing, but both my first nonfiction book and my first fiction book won writing awards. While awards may seem important to some, my purpose for writing is to educate, inspire, and correct misleading stories about Natives. Politics abound in the world of Native Studies; debates over authoritative voice and usefulness of writing swirl in every corner of the academy. "Popular" writing outside the academy is also scrutinized, honored, and criticized. It is a tough business indeed to write about Natives, but I am living proof that determination and self-education about writing can take you a long way.

I have written nine nonfiction and fiction books and edited four volumes about Natives, in addition to writing dozens of essays. As editor of the *American Indian Quarterly* (AIQ), I have encountered a spectrum of authors, who range from knowing precisely what we accept and how we prefer to receive submissions to those who obviously have no idea what *AIQ* publishes and are not familiar with professional protocol in submitting formal papers. As editor of the University of Nebraska Press's new book series titled Contemporary Indigenous Issues and a reader of dozens of submitted manuscripts over the past decade, I have also seen quite an array of proposed book manuscripts. Some are polished and thoroughly researched, while others appear disorganized, poorly written, and "retreaded," that is, the book is about a topic that has been written about repeatedly. I have seen and read a lot, enough to have a fairly good grasp of what works and what does not, and I have attempted to address these issues and more in this volume.

There is a lot in this slim book and all of it can relate to writing about Natives. While much of it is general information that could be used by any writer, the reality is that regardless of your subject – American Indians, Asians, bird watching, or architecture – you will go through the same experiences: agonies over writer's block and equipment malfunctions; frustrations over editing and reediting; elation at finally finding just the right sentence to complete a paragraph and then dejection at having a reader tell you it doesn't "work" (and then elation again when more readers say they love it); lengthy (and sometimes tedious) publication procedures; anxiety when waiting for book reviews; and peace when your writing flows. When I hear the word "writer" – with a Native focus or not – these are some of the things that come to mind. This book is not meant to discourage anyone from writing about Natives but rather to encourage sensitive, truthful, inclusive, and honest writing. If you do your research correctly, you will see the wealth of possibilities.

Note on Terminology

You will see that throughout the book I use the terms "American Indians" and "Natives" interchangeably. I sometimes use the former only because it is most recognizable to most Americans, but many Native people find the phrase offensive because it is a label assigned by Euro-Americans, not by the people themselves. I prefer "Indigenous" or "Native" (but not with "American") because both make a statement: Natives were created on this hemisphere and did not migrate from another continent. "Native American" refers to anyone born here, includ-

So You Want to Write about American Indians?

CHAPTER ONE

Think on These Things First

Writers must reflect on why they are using Native images and characters in their nonfiction and fiction stories. Is it to make money or to help with Natives' current situations? Out of respect and hopefully concern, Natives hope it's the latter.

There is always a market for original, well-written, thoroughly researched nonfiction and fiction. Many books written about Natives need revision so that tribes' viewpoints and voices are included. Desperately needed are problem-solving books and essays.

Teachers at all grade levels need intelligent, complete works that can assist them in properly educating their students about the diversity of Native America and the contributions Natives have made to this country and to the world.

Also needed are imaginative, inspiring, nonstereotypical fiction works about Natives. Both nonfiction and fiction can properly educate non-Indians about Native history and culture and can inspire, assist, and educate Indians themselves.

Are You Writing for Love or Money?

Before you get started on your project, ask yourself why you want to write about American Indians. Think carefully about these questions:
● Are you a student who must complete your thesis or dissertation in order to graduate?
● Are you a fiction writer who has ideas for a fiction novel or short stories?
● Are you a Native writer with a yearning to express yourself?
● Are you a professor who wants to make a name for yourself in your field of study?
● Are you a professor who must write in order to keep your job?
● Do you have visions of making money?

● Do you write for self-satisfaction?

● Are you someone who sees the myriad problems tribes face and would like to offer solutions through your writings?

There are dozens of examples of books that were written for all of the above reasons. Some are unique and inspiring, others are stereotypical, harmful to tribes, and of no use to anyone but the author.

If you're writing about Natives to make money, you may want to reconsider. Unless you have found what it is that mainstream America wants to read about American Indians – such as non-Native mystery writer Tony Hillerman or Native writers Louise Erdrich and Sherman Alexie – or you are a popular New Age writer (these writers often make their money unscrupulously by claiming to be "Indian shamans"), you probably won't make much monetary profit from your work. You may wonder how it is that some writers who don't write any better than dozens of other "nonfamous" Native writers can make so much money and get their names in *People* magazine and appear on NPR. The answer is they make a tidy profit because they have found a dynamite agent and publicist, are willing to promote themselves, and write what America wants to read.

Some of us who write scholarly works make a modest amount through royalties, but it is part of our jobs to write; we are paid primarily for our work as professors. Our promotion and tenure decisions are based in part on our publications. The adage "publish or perish" is very true in many instances and scholars must learn to write even if writing is not their primary career interest. Other nonscholarly writers might find success with a book or two, but most don't make enough money to quit their job.

Sure Ways to Make Money

Some people are under the impression that using Indian images and characters in their work will make it more attractive to readers; consider the popularity of *Dances with Wolves* and the Karl May and Hillerman novels; the images that helped form the foundations of the Boy and Girl Scouts, countless cartoons, and sports mascots; and desecration of burial sites. Most Americans and people around the world have always had a fascination with the original inhabitants of the Western Hemisphere.

Other writers, however, write because they want to, because they like the feeling of accomplishment completing a truthful, helpful book, essay, novel, or children's book can bring. If you are in this category, with few exceptions you will find it tough to make money. If you write critically about how Natives have been researched and written about and are an activist pushing for revisions to one-sided histories, then you will find grateful readers among most Natives, but your type of writing also will put you at odds with those who prefer to eschew Native viewpoints in favor of non-Native perspectives.

If you really want to make money, take as your example authors who have done the following:

• Write a stereotypical, biased work that includes no Native voices or perspectives and is patriotic in tone, that is, write about Indians in detail, but be sure to include "facts" that tell us white Americans were superior and tribes who lost lives, land, and culture really had it coming. Interestingly, another stereotypical and popular theme is the Bad White Man image that many readers like: show that all whites are evil that all Natives were innocent, childlike victims of the white onslaught.

• Write a fiction book that includes plenty of mystical characters who talk to animals and at least a few characters who are alcoholics and poverty-stricken. Ditto with a children's book that also includes plenty of pictures of Indians wearing braids and many animals mingling around; at least one animal must be perched on the Indian's shoulder.

• Write a children's book describing the major characters (one must be a grandpa) as having no sense of humor and whose life's purpose is to give advice to children who are confused about their identity, living in the city, going to the doctor, and so on.

• Write a book that tells about a certain tribe, replete with overblown details about poverty, alcoholism, and abuse, even if you really don't know about the tribe at all.

• Write a New Age book that reveals real or fabricated tribal religious secrets.

Realities of Writing about Natives

Besides the facts of money, there are other realities that anyone planning on focusing on Natives as a book or essay topic should know. These facts are undeniable, although many successful writers deny them anyway, mainly because they are usually writers who write the way the system (publishing houses, major professors, grant and award committees) wants them to. Many writers, especially those who adhere to the status quo (that is, the standard way of writing about Indians: not including Native viewpoints or Native versions of the past and present), have little difficulty finding outlets for their work. Native writers, on the other hand, often find the road to writing success bumpy at best. What I and many other writers have discovered are the following:

● Some of the controversies that are currently raging include
□ how books and essays should be written (objectively or subjectively)
□ what facts are the most reliable (written or oral testimonies)
□ who can better document the past and present (outsiders [non-Natives] or those who are more close to the topic [Natives with strong cultural connections and vested interest in the topic])
□ what the purpose is of writing about Natives (for profit, to assist tribes, or to do "comparative" works).
● Natives are misunderstood and misrepresented by the majority of people who write about them.
● Being "interdisciplinary," that is, utilizing techniques from a variety of fields to gather and analyze data, may be the most effective way of making sure you have included all information, but it still is not accepted by the old guard of scholars who demand that writers remain "discipline specific."
● There already are too many stereotypical books either biased in favor of white America (which means tribes are depicted as savage, uneducated drunks) or heavily slanted toward environmentally conscious, flowing-haired, nature-loving, ignorant savages of the wilderness. Indians can hardly recognize themselves in many works of nonfiction or fiction.

4

- The number of Native intellectuals is growing and they are challenging the way Natives are portrayed in fiction and nonfiction.
- Native writers who challenge the status quo in their writings have more problems getting published, graduating, and gaining tenure than those who support the colonial power structure.
- Many people have written nonfiction and fiction books without any adherence to research guidelines and without any concern about the tribes they focus on. Others believe that Natives are "fair game" and that they can write about any topic they choose without facing repercussions from the people they write about.
- Many writers write about topics that we have seen repeatedly; they often cite each other and incorporate no Native perspectives. Many Natives believe that there have been enough works written about them and that there is no need for further writings, except perhaps to offer suggestions for making their lives better.
- There are controversies over ethnic fraud. Only tribes decide who can be a member of their group, yet thousands of individuals claim to be Native for profit or for attention. For example, many writers continue to cite and quote the late Jamake Highwater because he claimed to be Blackfeet and hosted the television show *Primal Mind*. (Highwater's last name was actually Marks; he is Greek, not Native.) Many of the popular "Native" writers of fiction in the academy have questionable identities (that is, they cannot prove they belong to any tribe), yet because American Indian literary criticism is a field that does not do much in-depth questioning of writers' identities, many non-Natives who claim to be Indians gravitate to it.
- You must find ways to recognize stereotypes and bias in historical writings, including your own. Finding truthful information is critical to avoiding stereotypes.
- You cannot write a dry, repetitive, and unoriginal book and expect it to succeed. You must come up with new and different slants on common themes. Readers become bored very quickly and if you cannot hook them within the first five or ten pages, they will abandon your work for another.

Therefore, because of controversies over authoritative voice and usefulness in writing nonfiction and fiction:

- Expressing yourself is political.
- Writing about Natives is political.
- You are judged by what you write.
- There will be both good and bad consequences to writing about Natives.

These works explore the current controversies over writing about Natives:

Cook-Lynn, Elizabeth. *Anti-Indianism in Modern America: A Voice from Tatekeya's Earth.* Urbana: University of Illinois Press, 2001.

————. *Why I Can't Read Wallace Stegner and Other Essays: A Tribal Voice.* Madison: University of Wisconsin Press, 1996.

Mihesuah, Devon A. "Suggested Guidelines for Researchers Who Study American Indians." *American Indian Culture and Research Journal* 17:3 (1993): 131–39.

————, ed. *Natives and Academics: Discussions on Researching and Writing about American Indians.* Lincoln: University of Nebraska Press, 1998.

Mihesuah, Devon A., and Angela Wilson, eds. *Indigenizing the Academy: Transforming Scholarship and Empowering Communities.* Lincoln: University of Nebraska Press, 2004.

Smith, Linda Tuhiwai. *Decolonizing Methodologies: Research and Indigenous Peoples.* New York: Zed Books, 1999.

Your Challenges as a Writer

Acquiring a germ of an idea for a book or essay usually isn't difficult. But acting on those ideas and then sustaining that idea for an entire nonfiction or fiction work is. You must not only keep your interest so you can complete the thing and enjoy the process, you also must write clearly and provocatively enough to keep your readers interested in what you have to say. How can you meet these challenges with minimal stress?

BE ORGANIZED

A talent for writing is not the only tool you need to succeed. The topic must be thoroughly researched and put together in an organized and orderly fashion.

GET PERMISSIONS AND UNDERSTAND GUIDELINES

If you are a student, your thesis or dissertation must conform to the standards of your university, including your school's Institutional Research Guidelines. It also must be completed to the satisfaction of your major professor/adviser and to the tribe you are writing about. If you plan to submit your revised dissertation to a publisher, you also have to follow their guidelines.

DO YOUR RESEARCH

Research for nonfiction and fiction is time-consuming, tedious, and often stressful. Learning how to use the sometimes complex systems of a library, archive, museum, and the Web is only part of your education. You also must know how to interview Natives, how to ask permission to interview them, and how to consider the information you have found. You must learn how the social, political, religious, and economic aspects of American Indian life are interconnected. You cannot talk about the political aspects of a tribe without also considering how religion, gender roles, economy, worldview, and Euro-American policies affect tribal policies. Writers disassociated from tribal life do not understand how these issues interrelate, but this methodology makes perfect sense to Natives who are culturally aware.

LEARN METHODOLOGIES

Another serious debate in Native studies revolves around being "discipline specific," which means using only the methods of finding and analyzing data according to the tenets of your discipline (such as history, psychology, anthropology, etc.), or to be "interdisciplinary," meaning you use methods employed by a variety of disciplines to achieve a better, more well-rounded product. So, if you are a historian, you might use anthropological methods to find information and you may use data gathered by psychologists and biologists in your work. Many people who are anti-interdisciplinary argue that they do not believe that Native voices are accurate and they prefer to use only textualized data that they find in libraries. This stance is considered by many Natives to be racist because it purposely omits using Native voices.

7

KEEP READERS INTERESTED

In fiction writing, your work has to possess enough unique characters and situations to keep readers interested. Ineffective novels and short stories are those that have an uninteresting plot, little character development, and pervasive stereotypes. Nonfiction also must be creative and interesting enough to keep readers turning the page. Writers must choose a topic that has not been previously studied or must write about a familiar topic in a unique way. This is called creative nonfiction and all writers should learn how to write creatively.

EDUCATE

Good fiction and nonfiction about Natives must educate non-Indians about Natives, and it must be inspiring and educational to Natives.

BE SENSITIVE

Authors must be sensitive in what they write about. They must check with tribes to make certain that they do not overstep their bounds, and they must refrain from making overzealous judgments. It is your responsibility to learn stereotypes and to avoid them.

KEEP IN MIND THAT YOUR WRITING CAN AFFECT PEOPLE

Good examples of how Natives are strongly affected by books written about them are Laura Ingalls Wilder's Little House books. This series may be popular with non-Natives who know little about Natives, but for northern plains tribes who are portrayed as mindless savages who would best be exterminated, the books are stereotypical, insulting, and devastating to their self-esteem. My friend and Dakota writer Waziyatawiŋ Angela Wilson has spent much time protesting the Little House books. Why? Not only is she Dakota, but as a mother she must remain cognizant of what her three children read. What are her children supposed to think about how their tribe is depicted in these works of fiction? How can she protect her children from insults from other children after their teachers require these books to be read in the classroom? Why should she even have to worry about books such as these? As authors of works about Natives, we must make certain we are fair in what and how we write. Your published work about Native children won't disappear into a black hole and it can actually make an impact on someone.

What Do You Know?

I've lost count of the number of times a person has told me that he or she has read a certain book about Natives and thought it was great when I already knew that book is biased, includes no Native standpoints, and offers no new information to tribes. I've also encountered a good number of folks who ask me if a certain book is good because they found it on the shelves of Barnes and Noble. These people are similar to many of my students who write book reviews on works about Natives. They think that because a book has been published, has a neat cover, and has lots of endnotes that it must be reputable and truthful; otherwise, why would a publishing house take a chance on it?

Many think that because they've watched *Dances with Wolves*, read *House Made of Dawn*, were a Boy or Girl Scout, and have watched a powwow that they are knowledgeable about Native histories and cultures. While watching movies, reading novels, and listening to the music of flutist E. Carlos Nakai can spur your interest in Indigenous people, if you plan on writing about Natives, then you must know much more about them, such as the tribal history, how they dealt with Europeans, their language, religion, gender roles, appearances, politics, economies, and creation stories, and how they have survived to the present day.

Many authors pick out a tribe based on what they've seen in the movies, usually Apache, Comanche, or one of the Sioux peoples (who are invariably lumped into the same category) because Sioux are associated with tipis, braids, bison, and war paint, those things that most people think of when they read or hear the word "Indian." But these are only a few of the thousands of Indigenous groups that once inhabited the Western Hemisphere.

Say you have picked Apaches or Sioux to write about. Let's find out what you really know about them:

● Are you aware of the numerous groups that make up the larger term "Apache" (Mescalero, Membreno, Lipan, Chiricahua, Coyotera, Jicarilla, San Carlos, White Mountain, etc.) and "Sioux" (Lakota, Dakota, Nakota, Hunkpapa, Assinaboin, Oglala, Santee, Teton, Yankton, etc.)?

- Are you aware of where the tribe originally lived and where the groups migrated?
- How did these people historically see themselves in relation to the natural world, and how have those views changed throughout history up to today?
- Provided that you have permission to even hear them, what are their creation stories?
- What language do they speak?
- What were the traditional gender roles? How did they change because of colonization?
- What was their economy, that is, what did they eat in relation to the environment (beach, desert, plains, mountains, lush farmland)? Did they hunt, fish, forage, farm?
- What did their homes look like?
- What did the tribal people themselves look like (hair, skin color, height, bone structure)?
- What did they call themselves?
- How do they determine who are members of their tribe?
- What are the tribe's special relations with the federal government?
- What is treaty law and to what are the tribes entitled?

Tribal histories and cultures are vastly different from each other and are complex. Make certain you know the details. You can make a good start by reading these works: Nancy Bonvillain, *Native Nations: Cultures and Histories of Native North America* (New York: Prentice Hall, 2001); Duane Champagne, *Native America: Portrait of the Peoples* (Detroit: Visible Ink, 1994); Barry M. Pritzker, *A Native American Encyclopedia; History, Culture, Peoples* (New York: Oxford University Press, 2000); and Carl Waldman, *Atlas of the North American Indian* (New York: Facts on File, 1985).

What Time Period Are You Writing about?

Another serious consideration is the time period you are focusing on. Tribal cultures change with the times like other cultures, although the ways they change vary dramatically not only from tribe to tribe but also among individuals who make up the tribes. Indians do not live in a vacuum. They adapt, grow, and survive.

Consider the Cherokees. Cherokees living east of the Mississippi prior to removal in the 1830s lived differently from Cherokees who survived and made their home in Indian Territory, now Oklahoma. How are they different today from their brethren back in North Carolina? A full-blood Cherokee living in 1750 was considerably different from a modern Cherokee who might possess only 1/124 "Indian blood" and know nothing about their tribe. Do modern-day Cherokees look and behave in the same ways as their ancestors did in the 1880s? What about the 1850s? 1600s? Who speaks the Cherokee language today and who practices traditional religious ceremonies? Why do they believe what they do?

All of these aspects, at least, should go into your writing project. Natives are complicated peoples and unlike what many kindergarten teachers like to tell their students, Natives did not just live in the past, and they were – and are – not all alike. Listing all these factors might sound like an attempt to discourage you, but there are millions of tribally enrolled Natives in this country (and many more Natives in Central and South America), many of whom live in desperate, poverty-stricken conditions. Their histories are rich and complex and very different from each other. You are using their images for your benefit. You owe it to them to portray their lives correctly.

What Type of Book Will You Write?

There are a variety of markets for works on Natives. Scholars generally publish with university presses, although some work with larger publishing houses. Below are a few types of works to consider:

SCHOLARLY

The scholarly world of Native studies is different from the "popular" world. Scholarly works are authored by writers trained in specific disciplines. They are required to spend much time doing serious research about their topic and they have to explain their research methodology in the book. Scholarly works are critically reviewed by other scholars before the press editor makes a decision about accepting the work. Almost always, the author must complete revisions, some extensive, before the work is ready for publication. And even then, much of what is published is still unacceptable from a Native point of view. Scholarly books also are more limited in audience. These books are mainly found in libraries, but some that focus on popular topics make it into chain bookstores. The latter books are the ones that large publishing houses believe will make them money. Scholarly works also make money, but much less than popular works.

MASS MARKET

Mass market books are everywhere: grocery stores, truck stops, and newsstands, and they are price driven. These types of books are churned out as fast as possible in order to make a profit.

TRADE

Many books, such as Ruth Beebe Hill's *Hanta Yo* (Doubleday, 1979), a book that has insulted individuals in every Sioux tribe with her inaccurate portrayals of tribal life and culture, Ian Frazier's stereotypical book about life on Pine Ridge, *On the Rez* (Farrar, Straus and Giroux, 2000), or any of non-Indian Lynn Andrews's New Age books, would not pass muster among those who know tribal cultures well, which is one reason why authors like these avoided the rigorous academic review process and were published in the trade market. The other two reasons that authors often opt for a trade market publisher are that trade market editors know little about Indigenous people and will take anything well written, regardless of the content. Mainstream America also loves to read about stereotypes. Publishers of these kinds of books make much money and the readers are happy.

Who Will Read Your Work?

Not all readers read with the same motivations. Some want to be entertained, while others may want to learn something. Others, like scholars in a hurry to complete a research project, read to find specific facts. Some read to make certain that the book is not offensive.

GENERAL AUDIENCE

First and foremost, a general audience wants to be entertained. Many want to be educated, but they also want to look forward to what's on the next page. They don't care for in-depth arguments, endless footnotes, and scholarly-speak. This is the audience that can make you money, which is why many popular writers of Native topics avoid scholarly presses and do not use jargon.

YOUR MAJOR PROFESSOR AND THESIS OR DISSERTATION COMMITTEE

These individuals have a job to do in the academic realm, part of which is to make certain that you meet the standards of your discipline by composing a manuscript that shows your ability to research, organize, think, and write. You are supposed to state your thesis at the beginning of the project and then use the remainder of the manuscript to prove or disprove it. Academic exercises are supposed to be unique and they are usually the springboard to larger research topics. Smart students pick a thesis topic that has the potential to grow into a dissertation, and then into a book and spin-off essays. You must pick a topic that you like and are eager to investigate. Otherwise, the stress of graduate school will cause you to procrastinate and not complete the dissertation, rendering you yet another ABD (All But Dissertation) – meaning you have completed the requirements for your degree but haven't finished your dissertation.

A key to creating and finishing a product that you can be proud of is to choose a dissertation adviser who truly wants to help and support you. Avoid insecure professors who like to bully students into choosing certain topics or into using certain methodologies. These people read to make certain you have met the requirements all right, but they often can destroy your career if they don't like what you have written. Some professors use students for their own political agendas. If your major professor writes about the same topics you do, then make certain that your material is not used by that professor without your permission. This happens more than you might like to think. Choose wisely.

ACTIVISTS

Native activists are concerned about decolonization, nation-building, and empowerment strategies. They prefer works that include Native perspectives of history, and they want to see useful works that discuss how to better the lives of Natives. They have little patience for wannabes who claim to be Native and are not, repetitive literary criticism, and stereotypes. Indigenous activists will speak out against works that are biased and that use only non-Native points of view. Because activists are growing in number, all authors should be very aware that what they write will likely be scrutinized and criticized. If you don't do your job correctly, you might be exposed and discredited.

REVISIONISTS

Many activists are revisionists: that is, they reconsider what has been written and they are constantly looking for new information. One kind of revisionist wants to rewrite history so that the stories are told by Natives. Others are conservative and want stories to be more patriotic. Others may want to see less patriotism. The reason we see so many books on the same topics is because each author that comes up to the plate has a new interpretation, new sources, or a different belief system. They want to alter the works that have come before according to their interpretations.

TRIBAL MEMBERS

Like activists, most Natives connected to their culture want to read truthful histories and accounts of their cultures. They want to read about issues they are familiar with, but they want to know more. And they crave respectful work that discusses their tribe holistically, not just what the hunting males were doing at a certain time but also what duties and thoughts occupied the women, as well as other tribal members of all ages and socioeconomic levels. They want to read about fiction characters they recognize, identify with, and feel empowered by, which is why they do not read fiction by writers with no knowledge of Native life and culture.

Not all Natives are culturally aware, however, and they tend to believe everything they read, which is a major problem in itself. Some of these individuals suffer from the "boarding school syndrome" (BSS). They believe that "white is best" because they either learned that ideology in boarding schools or that idea was passed down through the generations to modern Natives from an ancestor who attended a boarding school. They don't object to stereotypes or sports mascots because they defer to all things dictated to them by white society. Activists are working hard to empower and educate those suffering from BSS. Be aware that not all Natives suffer from BSS; don't think that your work is adequate just because the one Native you know likes what you have to say.

NEW AGERS

The vast majority of New Agers are non-Indians who use bits and pieces of tribal chants, songs, and dances to create a sort of religion that is most definitely not Native. They tend to appropriate ceremonies, a mishmash of various tribes' sweat lodge rituals (they vary greatly in ritual and meaning from tribe to tribe) being the most popular. Many New Agers, such as Lynn Andrews, Harley Swift Deer Reagan, Rolling Thunder, Jamake Highwater, and many others are not Natives but claim they are to make money from ignorant followers who seek "enlightenment." New Agers seek out all books on Native culture, especially religion, to continue their creation of New Age culture.

SCHOLARS AND STUDENTS

A scholarly audience is a demanding one. They expect quality writing, thorough research, and provocative ideas. Students want facts and figures and they want the author to get to the point. Lists, bullets, and many summaries are especially welcome. They also like to argue with and challenge each other.

Many who write about Natives argue that they do not want to see politics in writing, but they will simultaneously argue against having Native voices and for using only non-Native sources. Those who do promote Native views in scholarly works can be just as aggressive in their demands. Both of these stances are, of course, political. You will receive robust praise or resounding criticism (even ostracism) depending on your political stance about writing and how you follow through with those beliefs in your writings. Scholarly writing can indeed be highly political and writers are often hampered by having to please the status quo instead of themselves so they can get a job, get promoted, or win grants. Adhering to the standards of the status quo when you don't really want to is called careerism, opportunism, and selling out and is a major problem in the academy.

Q & A

Q: *I'm a Native and consider myself to be an activist who is concerned about tribal issues, and I am concerned about finding a publisher for my works. Should I write what concerns me even though I know there will be many obstacles for me?*

A: Writers who challenge stereotypical or repetitive works and confront authors who do not consider Native perspectives will never be accepted by a good segment of scholarly writers. Members of the status quo who have been successful in writing about Natives solely from the white perspective and who are in charge of grant distributions, book awards, and promotion and tenure decisions may not know you, but they will dislike you nonetheless because you challenge their work and threaten their careers. Many non-Native writers (and some Native writers who subscribe to the status quo in order to be accepted) are concerned that they will lose control of Native studies if Native writers' concerns are taken seriously by the majority of people who write about Natives. As long as you are aware of the reality that you will have a tough row to hoe, then be true to yourself and write what is important. Plenty of people will appreciate you and genuinely want to hear your voice.

CHAPTER TWO

Stereotypes and Other Mistakes

For readers who are well aware of Native history and culture, reading a book replete with stereotypes is unbearable. Imagine how modern-day Natives feel when they read that their ancestors were "savages," "ignorant," or "heathens," or the countless other unsubstantiated stereotypical claims made by writers in thousands of books, essays, magazine articles, and children's stories. How do you think Native children endure classes taught by teachers who are woefully ignorant of tribal life but assert that Indigenous peoples are inferior to whites and continue to equate tribes with animals?

To make certain that your work is honest (you still have to verify the facts yourself), check your work carefully for the following stereotypes. Some are contained in the most popular movies about Native people and tribes that have emerged from Hollywood.

If you have included these stereotypes, then you're either aware of it and are using them to make money, or you aren't aware that these images are stereotypes. Either way, your work needs revision.

These stereotypes are covered more intensively in my book *American Indians: Stereotypes and Realities* (Atlanta: Clarity, 1996) in addition to Gretchen Bataille and Charles P. Silet, *The Pretend Indians: Images of Native Americans in the Movies* (Ames: Iowa State University Press, 1980); Aelene B. Hirschfelder, *American Indian Stereotypes in the World of Children* (Metuchen NJ: Scarecrow Press, 1982); and Raymond William Stedman, *Shadows of the Indians: Stereotypes in American Culture* (Norman: University of Oklahoma Press, 1982).

Indian Women Are Princesses

Thousands of Americans insist they have a "Cherokee Princess Grandmother." The claims are so pervasive that Natives have a name for it:

CPGS (Cherokee Princess Grandmother Syndrome). There were and are no "Indian princesses." This image was created by Europeans who, upon encountering Natives in the New World, desired to speak with kings. Tribal leaders were often seen in a comparable light and their daughters soon became known as princesses. This image also encompasses the stereotype of the "Indian maiden" as beautiful and willing to leave her tribe in order to marry any white man who came along.

If you have a female player, make certain she is not overly beautiful, willful, or lustful. If she does marry a white man, then include the rationalization for the union in clear terms. Sexual attraction is not the only reason most people get married, and that holds true for both Natives and whites.

Indian Women Are Squaws

If a Native woman is not beautiful and attracted to white guys, then she is the ugly, violent squaw who kills her enemies with more ferocity than her male counterpart. If you include a female such as this, then you had better include a justification for her behavior. If she is defending her land, tribe, and family, then she has good reason to behave in an angry fashion.

Native Women Are Unimportant

Women were and are active in every aspect of their tribes. Traditionally, women were powerful and respected. In Iroquois tribes, for example, women controlled the economy and the politics. Elder women decided when to declare war and when to stop it. They decided the fate of captives and they appointed the tribal leaders. In traditional Cherokee society, women decided how to punish transgressors. The problem for Native women came about with the invasion of missionaries, who preached that God is male and that men are superior to women. When white men started marrying Native women, European culture interjected itself into every aspect of tribal life, one result of which was the upheaval of traditional tribal gender roles. We have this stereotype because most histories written about Natives are authored by white men who had (and often still have) no appreciation for women's roles and preferred to focus on men.

18

Make sure that your work includes women when you discuss men. Native women did more than cook and clean. Research the tribe's gender duties to find out its political, social, religious, and economic roles at any given time period. Until recently, the important tribal roles of Native women have been ignored. In most books women are either mentioned not at all or only in passing as "the wife of." Kids' books usually feature a child and his relationship with a wise old man. It's almost as if women didn't exist in history, and we rarely read about them in a modern context. Not surprisingly, Sacajawea and Pocahontas get much attention mainly because they assisted white men. Today, there are more Native women politicians and more Native females enrolled in universities than ever before.

Look at these books for information about Native women: Paula Gunn Allen, *The Sacred Hoop: Recovering the Feminine in American Indian Traditions* (Boston: Beacon Press, 1986); Jennifer Brown, *Strangers in Blood: Fur Trade Company Families in Indian Country* (Vancouver: University of British Columbia Press, 1980); Devon Abbott Mihesuah, *American Indigenous Women: Decolonization, Empowerment, Activism* (Lincoln: University of Nebraska Press, 2003); Marla N. Powers, *Oglala Women: Myth, Ritual, and Reality* (Chicago: University of Chicago Press, 1986); Sylvia Van Kirk, *Many Tender Ties: Women in Fur-Trade Society, 1670–1870* (Norman: University of Oklahoma Press, 1980).

All Indians Are Bloodthirsty Savages

This image is one of the most common and pervasive. Movies and novels are filled with violent Native characters who mindlessly attack innocent whites. If you consider that many of those whites encroached onto lands that did not belong to them, utterly devastated tribal cultures, destroyed the peoples themselves, and broke every treaty they made with tribes, then some fighting back on the part of the Natives is only logical.

In order to rationalize taking the Western Hemisphere by force and deception, newcomers invoked the Doctrine of Discovery, a legal tradition based on the Crusades to the Holy Land, the holy wars that pitted Christians against "infidels and heathens." The ideology that

Christians have a God-given right to overtake non-Christian peoples continued to develop through the centuries and exists even today. If you consider the amount of violence generated by Christians in the name of God, then it is not hard to see that there is a bit of hypocrisy going on here.

Do not portray Natives as circling the wagons for no good reason, as Larry McMurtry does with the vile character Blue Duck in his otherwise wonderful *Lonesome Dove* (Simon and Schuster, 1985). Just because white folks show up on the plains doesn't mean Natives started salivating for their blood. If you present violent Indians, then show their side of the story. A good example of a missed opportunity was in the movie *Last of the Mohicans* (1992) in which the Magua character came across as irrational and violent. Further exploration would have revealed his sorrow and anguish over the loss of his family and his understanding that his culture might soon vanish, too. Many movies and novels need villains, but we also need their viewpoints. Conversely, do not portray white people as vicious demons bent on killing all Natives.

Natives Have No Religion

As we know most recently from current world events, controversies focusing on religion have brought about wars, suicide bombings, and terrorist attacks. From contact, non-Natives have rationalized their destruction of tribal America by claiming that Natives have no religion – that they are "heathens." In combination with the Doctrine of Discovery, Christians are able to justify and rationalize their violent, racist behavior against non-Christians. The reality is that traditional tribal cultures are strongly religious and, in fact, religion pervades every aspect of their culture.

Do not have Natives dancing around the fire whooping and hollering as though they do that on a daily basis. Tribal religions are complex and their ceremonies are intricate. Every song, dance, chant, and drumbeat has a meaning. Protocol must be followed, and not every member of the tribe was, or is, allowed to participate in every rite. Keep in mind that every tribe had a different religion, practiced in myriad ways. Don't tread into the deep jungle of religious discussion or even create a situation unless you have permission from the tribe's religious leadership to do so. Of course, if you are familiar with a tribe's religion, then you already know you should not discuss it.

All Indians Are Naturalists and Live in Harmony with (and, Conversely, All White People Sabotage) the Environment

The opposite of the heathen savage Indian is the gentle character who can speak to his friends (or hers, à la Pocahontas in the Disney version of part of her life before she died at age twenty-one in England) and the animals, morph into images of those pals, and meld into the environment while speaking wisely about how we should treat the earth, etc. Of course, tribes knew a lot about the earth because they had to live with her. Out of necessity they learned about food, what could be used as medicine, and that if one harvests too many plants or animals then the supply runs short. But Natives were and are not natural-born ecologists.

If you place Natives in an outdoor setting, don't have them change into animals unless you are quite familiar with stories about witchcraft. Natives don't have a monopoly on talking to animals – many people do that – and having them carry on a meaningful conversation is treading on stereotypical ground.

Natives Desire Outsider Participation in Their Religious Ceremonies, and They Like Having Their Pictures Taken and Voices Recorded by Strangers

Unlike many American religions that proselytize and go door-to-door trying to garner new recruits and converts, tribal peoples (and they are all different) do not try and recruit people to their tribal faith. They value privacy and expect outsiders to respect those wishes. This means Natives do not want anyone observing their ceremonies, and they do not take kindly to New Agers who want to take bits and pieces of their songs and dances and cobble together a "religion" that is unrecognizable to Natives. Although some writers have made a good deal of money writing about tribal religions, no one but Natives should write about their private cultural information. Some scholars manage to educate readers about Native religions without revealing their sacred aspects.

21

All Natives Live on Reservations

We can blame moviemakers for causing millions of Americans to believe that all Indians are alike. While some tribes did historically live in tipis (some individuals live in tipis for part of the year or during certain ceremonies), wore braids, and rode horses on a regular basis, the majority of tribes did not live on the plains. Tribes from North to South America lived in a variety of homes including wooden homes with shingles and chimneys, wickiups, plank houses, pueblos, and earth lodges. Hair styles vary from tribe to tribe and range from braids to "Mohawks" to loose hair worn unadorned to their ankles. Any wildlife book on bison shows that their range did not extend across the continent. Many Natives in the past never even saw bison, much less hunted them.

Make sure that the cultural aspects you use are accurate. Most tribes did not wear headdresses or braids. Many museum archives, such as the Smithsonian Institution in Washington DC, the Amon Carter Museum of Western Art in Fort Worth, Texas, the Oklahoma Historical Society in Oklahoma City, and dozens of state historical societies and university special collections house thousands of photographs. Look at those before you proceed with details about Natives' appearances. There are things to keep in mind when using photographs. Many pictures were staged by a photographer who desired to have his subjects looking as "Indian" as possible: holding war clubs, wearing feathers, and dressing stereotypically. Assessing the authenticity of photographs is a major undertaking.

Informed readers are eager to read your accurate descriptions. However, they will catch any errors, no matter how small. Specifics are what give your work life and importance, and it will take effort on your part to make certain that you have your descriptions correct. Don't take shortcuts and try to generalize.

A look at any ten fiction books featuring Natives will probably show that the Native characters are all alike. How would mainstream fiction survive if all white characters looked, acted, and thought alike and, worse, had the exact same motivations? Readers wouldn't tolerate this kind of poor character development, so keep in mind that Native readers don't tolerate monolithic Native characters either, which is why they don't usually buy fiction focusing on Natives unless they are familiar with the author.

All Indians Want to Be Called "Indian"

"Indian" is a Euro-American term and so are "American Indian" and "Native American." Each tribe has its own name and that is what they prefer to be called. But beware. There are often several names for each tribe. Cherokees, for example, are Tsalagi. Choctaws are Chatas. Navajos are Dinee.

When referring to tribes in a general sense, "Indian" is the most recognizable. But that does not mean it is the most acceptable. Activists prefer "Indigenous" because it makes a strong statement about where they believe tribes emerged (from North America, not in the Old World), or "First Nations" if they're from Canada.

If you plan to write about a specific tribe, then you must consider whose perspective you're using when you write, as well as the time period. If you write about Ho Chunks yet consistently refer to them as Winnebagos (unless you include a character that doesn't know better and calls them "Winnebago"), you'll lose credibility immediately. If you write about Apache, Iroquois, or Sioux tribes, then you have to be specific.

If you write nonfiction, you must explain at the outset why you use certain terminology. You need to know the political ramifications of using "Indian," "Native American," "First Nations," and "Indigenous."

Real Indians Lived before Reservations

Thanks to Hollywood, moviegoers are under the impression that all Natives lived in the past and none exists today. Even for many people who do know that there are almost four million Natives in America right now, they view them as merely pale imitations of their more glorious tipi-living, horse-riding, and war paint–wearing ancestors. Know the demographics of your subjects. That means current populations of tribes, as well as enrollments of Natives in school, in the military, etc. Look at the Web sites of tribes and read about their services and social activities. It may take you a while, because throughout the United States and Canada, tribes have created informative and lengthy Web pages that detail the activities of their current lives.

All Natives Are Rich from Casinos

Some tribes – most notably the Pequots – have made some money from casinos on their tribal lands. But the reality is that the majority of tribes do not have casinos on their lands. Even those that do often do not make as much money as the non-Native investors who helped them build the casino. The number of Indian casinos is growing, as is the literature that focuses on the topic. Don't write that every tribe makes money from casinos when not every tribe has one.

All Natives Are Drunks

All it takes is for tourists to see one drunken Indian and they assume that all Indians drink. While some Natives do drink, not all of them do. There is no evidence to back the claim that Natives have a physiological tendency toward alcoholism. An alcoholic Native character is so common that it's unusual not to include one. Here's a good strategy to get you to notice how much of this type of writing you're doing: for every drunken Native you plan to include in your book, be sure to include a drunken white person.

If Natives Had Cooperated with Each Other, They Could Have Prevented Euro-American Colonization

This is an interesting hypothetical situation. Perhaps if all the residents of the New World had come together to ward off the intruders, the invasion could have been delayed. However, because tribes lived hundreds of miles apart, had no means of communication (plus their languages were and are different), and horses were not introduced until the mid-1500s in Mexico (and it took another two hundred years for them to make their way to the northern part of the area we today call the United States), there is no way the tribes could have known about one another – much less gotten together to cooperate – long enough to repel the initial invaders. In addition, with the cultural differences and animosities among tribes, who would have been in charge?

Natives Were Defeated Because They Were Weak and Stupid

Natives did not almost become "a vanished race" by 1800 because they were weak. Even if the tribes banded together, they would have fallen quickly to the diseases to which they had no immunity. Millions of Natives in North and South America were killed quickly by diseases, most notably smallpox, whooping cough, and measles brought from the Old World. Their mental capacities had nothing to do with the destruction of their cultures and populations.

Natives Had No Civilization until Euro-Americans Brought Their Ideologies to Them

Webster's dictionary defines "civilization" as the following: 1. a relatively high level of cultural and technological development: the stage of cultural development at which writing and the keeping of written records is attained; 2. the process of becoming civilized; 3. refinement of thought, manners, or taste.

Considering that Natives did not have a written language (Cherokees were the only ones who developed a syllabary, and that was not until 1821; tribes have been passing down their histories and cultural knowledge for centuries, but they have done it orally) and that Euro-American society was socially (including male and female roles), economically, religiously, and politically different from tribal cultures, it is no wonder the invaders believed themselves superior to the Natives. The conflict occurred because tribal cultures were different from European cultures. That tribes were not Christian only added to the Europeans' rationalization that they were superior and civilized and that the tribes deserved to be subsumed.

Natives Arrived in the Western Hemisphere by Traversing the Siberian Land Bridge

There is no proof to support this theory of migration from the Old World. Hundreds of tribes have creation stories that say they were created in this hemisphere, either underground and they emerged onto the surface, or underwater. While many non-Natives view these stories as quaint "myths," do not ignore the fact that Natives are entitled to their versions of creation and those versions should be included in any work that discusses origins.

Natives Have Nothing to Contribute to the World

Take a look at the names of places, foods, and war veterans (it is estimated that one in four Native males is a veteran), including code talkers from a dozen tribes, and the reality that Natives participate in every facet of American life. Foods such as tomatoes, potatoes, cacao, avocados, raspberries, manioc, squashes, maple sugar, corn, and pumpkins contributed to the dramatic population increase throughout the world after they were introduced to the Old World. Many scholars argue that the federal government is in part patterned after the political organization of the Iroquois Confederacy. And don't forget that Native images serve as fuel for countless books, essays, and movies, resulting in lucrative careers for non-Natives.

All Natives Are Patriotic

It doesn't take much in-depth reading of America's history of land grabbing, treaty breaking, and outright killing combined with present-day racism to understand why Natives might be loath to salute the American flag. Although many Natives serve in the armed forces (they have participated in every war the United States has fought), most of them fought to defend their tribal lands. While a lot of patriotic Americans are angry that some Natives appear to be anti-America, keep in mind that many Americans are anti-Indian, which puts those Natives in the tough position of living on their tribal lands in the midst of a racist country.

All Natives Get a Free Ride from the Government

Any Native who has attended a university has probably heard the claim that all Indians get scholarships. Many others are surprised to hear that they receive free cars, trucks, houses, health care, and food in addition to monthly checks for undisclosed amounts of money. It is true that some tribes receive annuities from the government and some individuals receive money; this is because of treaty agreements the tribe made with the federal government in exchange for giving up vast amounts of land. In other words, some Natives are still being paid for what was taken from them. Not all Natives receive money from the government, and many struggle to survive in the worst possible situations.

Natives' Affairs Are Managed for Them by the Bureau of Indian Affairs

Because tribes have their own governments – many of which are complex – they manage their own affairs, including education, health care, social services, environmental protection, economic development, housing, and road maintenance. Some manage better than others, but all appear to be making efforts to achieve true sovereignty – the ability to govern themselves without interference from the federal government.

Natives Are Too Stupid to Complete School

This belief is still pervasive, referring to Natives at all grade levels, even through graduate school. Ironically, some of us hear that we graduated from university and get our books published only because we are Natives and owe our success to affirmative action. Not only do hundreds of Natives earn their terminal degrees each year on their own merits, Natives excel in every grade and win academic scholarships. And many of them do it while maintaining strong ties with their tribal cultures. While it is true that some Natives are passed through school, the same can be said about students of every other race and of both genders.

Natives Cannot Vote or Hold Office

In 1924, the Indian Citizenship Act gave citizenship to all Natives who had not already been made citizens by treaty agreements and statutes or who were honorably discharged in World War I. Cherokees, Choctaws, and Sioux have served in Congress; Charles Curtis, a Kaw, was

Herbert Hoover's vice president; Northern Cheyenne Ben Nighthorse Campbell and numerous members of other tribes have served in the Senate. Last year three Navajos were elected to the Arizona state legislature. Dozens of Native women hold political office. The list goes on.

Most Americans Have an Indian Grandparent

Many Americans claim to have a Cherokee grandmother (occasionally she's from another tribe, but Cherokee seems to be the tribe of choice). Many people "self-identify" as Indian, but this is not a legitimate classification. "Indian" is defined in various ways. Tribes recognize as members only those people who are enrolled in that tribe. And you become a member of that tribe by meeting its membership criteria, which vary from tribe to tribe. You must ask the tribal registrar for those guidelines. The U.S. government recognizes as Indians those people who are enrolled in a state or federally recognized tribe and have at least one quarter Indian blood. If you want a scholarship from the BIA, you must be tribally enrolled and one quarter Indian blood. If you are not tribally enrolled, the odds are stacked against you that anyone will believe you're Indigenous. There are very, very few exceptions to this rule, although countless wannabes continue to argue that self-identification as Indians should be an appropriate way to determine who is Native.

All Natives Are Full-Bloods

The vast majority of Natives are of mixed heritage: that is, they have non-Natives in their background or they have a person from another tribe as an ancestor. Many Natives are "full-blood mixed-bloods": they have grandparents from four different tribes. Some enrolled Natives are blond and blue-eyed. There is a difference, however, between being racially Native and being culturally aware. Although some people balk at mixed-heritage peoples' claim to Indianness, as long as they are enrolled in a federally recognized tribe they are legitimate members of that tribe. Whether culturally aware Natives care to include those culturally unaware Natives in their lives, however, is another story.

All Indians Are Mixed-Bloods

Because most Natives are mixed-bloods (there are some Cherokees who are one two-thousandth Cherokee blood), many people assume they all are. It is also one reason why so many people claim to be Native. If Chuck Norris, Kim Basinger, Heather Locklear, and Val Kilmer can claim to be Native and get away with it, then why can't legions of other blond people? In a fiction novel I read last year for a writer's contest, an author included the requisite "half-blood" character who possessed "tawny" skin and blue eyes. Writers must research the genetic possibility of a person acquiring blue eyes after only one generation of intermarriage between a full-blood Native and a Caucasian. This scenario simply is not possible, nor is it probable that a blond, blue-eyed, light-skinned person has a "full-blood Cherokee grandmother."

All Natives Have an "Indian Name"

Probably the most comical stereotype is the Indian character who has an Indian name that is part animal, part color, and/or part force of Nature: Black Wolf, Red Thunder Eagle, etc. Some real Indians do have these kinds of names, but they were given for a reason. Mihesuah, for example, is Comanche for "first to fight." Many other Natives did not translate their names into English.

Native and non-Native readers who are informed about tribal names are aware of what is realistic and what is not. While it is true that some Natives have "Indian names," those names are not for public knowledge and you'll never know what they are. If you plan on using a Native character in your novel, you would do well to look at the Dawes Rolls at list names of Cherokees, Choctaws, Creeks (Muscogees), Chickasaws, and Seminoles. You may be surprised to see that during the late 1800s, at least, stereotypical names were almost nonexistent. See the Index to the Final Rolls of Citizens and Freedmen of the Five Civilized Tribes in Indian Territory (Dawes) at the Oklahoma Historical Society, Indian Archives Division in Oklahoma City, or at the Federal Archives in Washington DC, and in Fort Worth, Texas.

Natives Know the Histories, Languages, and Cultural Aspects of Every Tribe

This goes hand-in-hand with the belief that "all Indians are alike," so why shouldn't we all know about each other? Many Natives don't know about their tribe, much less about others. They do not all necessarily get along with each other either.

Natives Have No Sense of Humor

Non-Natives get this impression because out of respect, Natives tend to be reserved around strangers. The old photographs we see of Natives were taken after treaty signings, hardly an occasion to smile. The majority of children's books about Natives depict the characters as completely humorless. Most people would agree that a stoic and unsmiling grandpa or grandma, not to mention a parent, is a truly scary individual; yet we are subject to this type of dull personality in countless works of history and kids' stories.

A Few More Vocabulary Dos and Don'ts

● Use the word "different" to describe the cultures of Natives and Euro-Americans. The word "uncivilized" is racist and incorrect.

● Tribal creation stories should not be referred to as "myths" because this implies that the stories are made up, whimsical, and not true. Use "stories" instead.

● Never say that Indians are "heathens" simply because many are not Christians. Use "Indians are religious" instead.

● Terms such as "squaw," "buck," "papoose," and "Ca Manch" (the term John Wayne used to describe Comanches) are all incorrect and insulting. Refer to Natives as you would anyone else – "man," "woman," "child" – and don't use slang just because you can't pronounce their tribal name.

● No Natives had or have red skin. Don't use the term "red man."

● Natives rode and ride "horses" not "ponies."

● "Half-breed" is a term used to describe dogs. Like the "N-word" some use to refer to blacks, "half-breed" is insulting, even though sometimes Natives use it among themselves. Outsiders and writers should use "mixed heritage."

CHAPTER THREE

Getting Started with a Project and Staying with It

You know your potential audience and you now have an inkling of an idea of what to write about, but you still aren't sure. How do you go about solidifying your idea and keeping your enthusiasm? Here are some things that you must do as you gear up for your writing project.

Read for Knowledge

In order to garner ideas for your project and to decide how to write it, you must read works that pertain to your topic and inspire you. Most successful writers read in order to learn their craft. Never stop reading, even if you're in the midst of a project. Reading is time-consuming and you may think you have no extra minutes in the day, but keep in mind that reading is part of the foundation of scholarship and of being a writer. If you don't read, don't expect to go very far.

If you are not a Native then you must read about Natives. Even if you are Native and know quite a bit, you must read to supplement your (presumed) knowledge about your tribe's history and culture. This does not, however, mean that you should believe everything you read. Many works are poor, while others are quite good; you must be aware of both kinds – this is what makes you an informed reader. Not only must you look at scholarly works, you also must read articles, newspapers, book reviews, commentaries, and first-person accounts. If you have access, listen to those who have stories to tell you. In addition, read books that critically analyze other books. You also must read to learn what has already been published and what the various publishing houses are interested in taking.

Keep this in mind: if you decide to write about a Native, or a tribe – even in passing – then you must be as informed as you possibly can be about that person or tribe. There always will be others, namely Natives and many non-Natives who have spent a good portion of their lives interacting with tribes, who are more knowledgeable than you about your topic. This does not mean that all people claiming to be Native or "part Indian" know everything about Natives; unless they have interrelated with their tribe and have spent their lives actually living as Natives, then they have to read and research, too. Most Natives, however, are aware of stereotypes because we have to live with them.

Choosing a Topic

Most writers pick a topic they are interested in or a group of people they grew up next to, or the writer is Native and is concerned about an issue that directly affects him/her and his/her tribe. There are several things to think about as you consider a nonfiction or fiction topic:

● Is the topic useful? Can everyone, including tribes, learn from it?

● Is there enough information on the topic? Library archives are one source of written information, but the tribal versions are another. You must use both. Otherwise, if you are an historian who refuses to use tribal sources, for example, you have to answer Native historian Waziyatawiŋ Angela Wilson's question about the type of work you've produced: "American Indian History or White Versions of American Indian History?"

● Make certain there is not too much information. If the topic has been researched numerous times you might be "plowing familiar ground"; you need to find something else. Some overresearched topics include Custer, Cherokees, sun dances, Comanches, Indian wars, identity, and Indian captivity.

● Can you secure tribal permission for your topic? If you are doing a serious study of a tribe, you cannot do the work adequately without conversing with knowledgeable members of that tribe. Will they talk to you? Better to find out before you get started than to have a rude awakening after you've been working on your project for six months. Many Hopis, for example, are suspicious of anyone writing about them and will rarely talk to outsiders.

● For academics: Have you sent your project proposal through your university's Institutional Review Board IRBto ensure that you are following correct research protocols?

● For every writer: Have you checked with the tribe's research guideline committee? Have you checked to see if the tribe you are writing about has tribal research guidelines? Many tribes who are weary of being the focus of books and essays have instituted guidelines in an effort to more closely monitor what is being written about them. The Cherokee, San Carlos Apache, and Hopi tribes are just a few who want researchers and writers to check with them to make sure their project is appropriate.

How to Find What Has Been Written

Students and nonacademics often know what they want to write about; they just have no idea how to go about it. Once you find your topic, what are the next steps? There are numerous places to look. Start with the back issues of the journals listed below (they are available at most university libraries) and be sure to look at the book review sections:

● *American Indian Culture and Research Journal*
● *American Indian Quarterly*
● *Ethnohistory*
● *Wicazo Za Review*
● *Western History Quarterly*

Next, search for your topic in the following places:
● your local university library's catalog
● http://www.alltheweb.com or another good search engine
● http://www.amazon.com
● http://www.developmentgateway.org/ for information about the latest research in the areas of traditional knowledge and problem solving
● Social Sciences directory

These books also contain helpful bibliographies on topics dealing with Natives:

Bataille, Gretchen, and Kathleen M. Sands, eds. *American Indian Women: A Guide to Research*. New York: Garland, 1991.

———. *American Indian Women: Telling Their Lives*. Lincoln: University of Nebraska Press, 1984.

Miller, Jay, Colin G. Calloway, and Richard A. Sattler. *Writing in Indian History, 1985–1990.* Norman: University of Oklahoma Press, 1995.

Prucha, Francis Paul. *A Bibliographical Guide to the History of Indian-White Relations in the United States.* Chicago: University of Chicago Press, 1977.

―――. *Indian-White Relations in the United States: A Bibliography of Works Published 1975–1980.* Lincoln: University of Nebraska Press, 1982.

Looking at these sources will tell you if there is enough material to even get started and if your topic has been done repeatedly. If it's the latter, you want to make certain that your slant on the topic is different from what everyone else has done. Not only that, you need to consider whether that topic is useful or merely a "curiosity piece" that won't benefit anyone but you. This is an ethical consideration and an important one.

Ask If It Is an Appropriate Topic

You now must find out if writing about this topic is acceptable to tribes. Many religious topics are taboo, as are other related sensitive cultural topics such as ceremonies, clan relations, and familial histories. Unless you plan on becoming a writer with a reputation for having no concern for the people you write about (and that includes many prominent, award-winning writers), then you should contact tribes to see if they approve of what you are doing. You must start early. Don't decide on a topic on Monday and plan to start that afternoon. Think of a topic in April and get an answer about it in July.

Organization

The more organized you are, the smoother your writing project will be. Everyone has his/her own system for organizing material and a schedule for writing and editing. After earning four university degrees and spending fifteen years as a professor, I know that the time invested in organization and planning is crucial to success as a nonfiction and fiction writer. I recommend that all writers, especially scholars, buy a filing cabinet and stock it with file folders. I have a file for every lecture and every topic I have written about. I drop in newspaper articles, essays that I find or that others send to me, and interesting pieces that pop up on the Web. For example, I had one file labeled "Methodology," but over the years that has branched out to many subfiles, including "Oral History," "Controversies," and "History of Ethnohistory." Book contracts, reading lists, syllabi, and grant applications all go into files labeled with those headings.

Because I've been interested in repatriation of Indian sacred cultural objects and skeletal remains, since the early 1980s I had collected hundreds of essays, books, newspaper clippings, and pamphlets dealing with the topic. When it came time to put together my book on repatriation, I had an impressive amount of information to help me put the issue in perspective. The same goes for my books on stereotypes, methodologies about writing, Indigenous women, and fitness and diets, as well as my essays on identity and historiography. I also have boxes of information divided up according to my fiction topics.

How you dispose of all that information when you are through is another story. I tend to give much of my research data to colleagues and students who work on the same topics. The mounds of data I collected for my work on the Cherokee Female and Male Seminaries, for example, has gone to Northeastern State University in Tahlequah, the university that grew out of the Cherokee Female Seminary.

Your organization for specific writing projects will determine whether you get through the experience smoothly. If you are not organized properly, you will become stressed because you cannot find the documents you mislaid, you cannot think of what to write next, and you may have no idea how to start the project. There are some tools you can use to make the process smoother, although it does take work to get them in place. Once you do, you will be a happier writer.

Note Gathering

For the library portion of your research there are several ways to approach gathering notes. The most effective and useful way is also the most time-consuming. Buy several hundred 3 x 5 cards and for every "fact" you find, write it on a card. On the top line of the card write the citation.

> Mihesuah, Devon. American Indigenous Women p. 102
> "The two most prevalent images of Native women – the princess and the squaw drudge – still affect Native women's self-esteem."

If you find many useful factoids in one book, use a code to identify the book, but do not forget to write down the page and volume number. There is nothing worse than losing the author's first name or another vital detail that must be included. Sometimes names and volumes can be recovered through Web searches, but you certainly do not want to revisit that library in Madrid to find a lost page number on a document confined to the archives.

Make a separate card with bibliographic data (author, title, publisher, date of publication, etc.) on it for every source you use so you have a stack of source cards that you can later alphabetize.

> Mihesuah, Devon Abbott
> American Indigenous Women: Decolonization, Empowerment, Activism
> Lincoln: University of Nebraska Press, 2003

You will find this makes it easier for you when it comes time to type your bibliography or references cited list. Some writers complain about the volume of cards they generate, but the upside is multifold. You can arrange the facts in the order you want according to your outline. Use a sturdy shoebox with dividers to signify your chapters. You can use the cards again for other related projects and to index your book, then you can use the backside of the cards for your next project.

For my book on the Cherokee Female Seminary, I made a card for each seminary student (over two thousand) and on each card put all the demographic data I accumulated on each student. Combined with the cards I made for all the other data, such as an overview of the complex Cherokee history, I had thousands of cards (with one fact on each card). Doing it this way was invaluable for compiling the demographics, making the bibliography, and using the information for a few future projects such as the Cherokee Male Seminary and essays on identity, boarding schools, and women.

Another strategy is more advanced but effective if you're an experienced writer. Make copies of all the written data you find (yes, it gets expensive, but at least you don't have to sit and copy it from a book onto a card). Arrange the papers into the order you intend to write the book (each chapter should have its own file), and compose the manuscript on your computer as you read through the pile. This requires much planning so you know what you're going to write, although I've seen one writer without an outline create his book as he read the data.

Why Outlines?

Many writers shun making outlines because they believe they make the writer feel trapped, that he/she must adhere to that outline no matter what. Others resist making outlines because they are not easy to create. While some writers can get away with not making outlines for a few projects, most projects require at least a skeletal outline. Most students will at one time or another encounter a professor who requires an outline, so you may as well jump in and learn to create one.

Once you have all your data, think about how you should organize the manuscript or essay. After you have read many books and essays, taken pages of notes, and found piles of documents, you need to get them in order. What has worked for me is to put all information on a particular chapter either in a file or in an accordion folder, depending on how much I have. This at least gets all the paper and cards off your floor. For my book on the female seminary, I purchased several metal boxes to hold the note cards and used cardboard dividers to signify chapters. I also had files of paper. Although I had a complicated system of finding information, being organized was crucial to knowing where information was located.

After you have the information neatly arranged, you can go into each chapter file and organize it into more detailed order. While some people think it excessive, you may need to make two copies of one document or set of notes to put in more than one file because the topic overlaps and you can't decide where it goes. This way, you won't lose the topic idea when you go from file to file.

Experienced writers pretty much know what their outline might look like and already have one in mind as they gather data; however, that outline varies as they find more information so you should never feel like you are glued to your first idea or first outline draft. As you accumulate information you are really gathering more ideas. Changing your mind about how to present your findings is inevitable.

When you are first thinking about a project, use a yellow pad or notebook and a pencil (so you can erase easily when you change your mind about minor issues) to jot down your initial ideas about the project. If you're a student with an idea for a term paper, thesis, or dissertation, write down all the ideas you have, including the theme, subtopics, key words, and possible titles. All of these will change a lot or a little, but these initial ideas are crucial so don't throw anything away. I keep a separate file labeled "Ideas" where all my initial notes go. If I can't use an idea for one project, I often find a use for it in another project.

Ways to Sort Your Information

Depending on your topic, you can organize in several different ways:

● *Data according to the date* (not the date you found it, the date the event occurred). For long historical projects it helps to initially organize your data from the earliest event to the most recent. But this is only the first step. You may have your data arranged according to when it happened, but you also need to have the thematic material in there someplace. Some writers write down theme possibilities on separate pages that correspond with each time period. Before you begin writing, you should go through the data and attach a page or so of how you interpret that historical data. For example, in my biography of my father-in-law, Henry Mihesuah, I had hundreds of transcribed pages about his ancestry, childhood, education, service as a Marine, and life as a relocatee in California. Putting all this into chronological order seemed the logical way to organize the book, but it was not as interesting or informative as the final version, in which I arranged the work according to theme (and not all of it was put into chronological order) and incorporated my discussions of those themes at the start of each chapter.

• *Data according to theme.* This probably works best for those who do non-history topics. For the long, complicated essay I wrote on identity choices and development ("American Indian Identities: Comment on Issues of Individual Choices and Development," *American Indian Culture and Research Journal* 22:2 [1998]: 193–226), I initially accumulated three file boxes of data. Some were lecture materials and were already in labeled files. Other pieces were journal articles. I didn't have as many books as I use in history projects, but I did use a dozen dissertations. I organized all this into piles, each pile a separate theme, such as definitions, ethnic fraud, appearance, importance of studying identity, and so on. Some overlapped, so I separated the obvious topics first. But a laundry list of topics containing separate chunks of information is not always interesting. I had to find ways to integrate the various themes and issues so the essay remained compelling from start to finish. One way to accomplish that is to incorporate real-life situations with which the readers can identify. In this case I used "Life Stages" as proposed first by African American scholar William Cross as a base and an outline, then used Native issues as comparative examples (this is where interdisciplinary research comes in). Using bullets and subheadings makes reading easier. Many readers have commented that this format was logical, understandable, and enjoyable because they could identify with many of the examples. This complex essay, however, went through a dozen rewrites before I was satisfied that it was comprehensible enough to show to another reader.

How to Keep Your Enthusiasm

So you have spent countless hours in the library and archives, talked to informants, and listened to recorded interviews. You've met with the reference librarian, surfed the Web, and built piles of paper and books in your office and maybe throughout your house. You have your thesaurus, dictionary, atlas, and editing book within reach. So why are you not writing?

Through the years I've heard many faculty members ask how they can complete their book in time for their tenure review. Graduate students ask in panicked voices for strategies to help them finish their dissertation in order for their committee to read it so they can graduate. Nonacademics just want to know how to write and find a publisher, period. Many who do write often get bored, frustrated, and anxious. They claim to suffer from "writer's block" and are unable to find inspiration. Other activist writers become discouraged at the consistent resistance to their works and have little desire to continue writing.

Countless unproductive writers say they'll start on this or that project "after I move," "after my surgery," or "after I reshingle my roof." And, of course, they come up with another reason not to get started after the old excuse wears thin. This is called procrastination and regardless of whether you feel fat, angry, or hungover, if you really want to write, then you have to write. If you really do not want to write then admit it to yourself and stop talking. Otherwise, you'll become a master procrastinator armed with endless excuses.

Instead of waiting until the time is "perfect" to write (which will never arrive), try to use your anger, frustration, and head pain to create something interesting and unique. I've done my most successful writing when I'm mad.

There is only one way to complete your manuscript and that is to write it. No amount of wishing will make it happen unless you PBIC (Put Butt in Chair). Writing a first draft might be painless and even enjoyable, but the hard part – and where the majority of your energy will be spent – is in editing your work. Many writers revise a manuscript or essay a dozen times before they're somewhat satisfied with their product. Students should recruit colleagues to help them edit their work and not rely on their roommates who may know nothing about writing techniques.

You must be consistent. You must set aside time each day to put pen to paper or fingers to keyboard. Writing takes determination and discipline. Some people juggle family, work, and the basic daily chores and only have a small amount of time to write each day. If you have only half an hour in the morning, then use it. If you find ten minutes while dinner is cooking, then write something. My major professor at Texas Christian University (TCU), Don Worcester (a prolific writer of history and fiction novels), always told me "a page a day is a book a year." While there is more to writing than writing down your thoughts (such as the incredibly time-consuming data gathering, contemplating, and editing), this comment about being consistent says it all.

If you plan on writing for a career, or if writing is part of your career, then it is crucial to make the opportunities to write. Writers with children must find child care and they must organize their time. I am constantly asked how it's possible that I've written fourteen books in fourteen years when my commitments are many: I'm a professor, journal editor, mother of two small kids, and sled-dog racer, and I work out everyday (and I don't have a housekeeper). The answer is simple: I am highly motivated, I don't waste time, and I write everyday, even if it's in a journal so that I can transfer those writings to the computer at another time. I read newspapers, novels, and submissions to *American Indian Quarterly* while riding my recumbent bicycle and on the step machine. When I run and hike in the mountains by my home (where I do a lot of thinking), I take a small notebook in my fanny pack and write down any pertinent thought about a project. I have a thesaurus, dictionary, several books on editing, and an answering machine, and I *use* them. It is hard for me to concentrate on writing at my university office, so I use any time I have outside of classes, meetings, and student discussions to outline and edit. I write at home.

To make the process of writing more pleasant, my computer is situated by my home office window where I can look out at the birds, squirrels, forest, and my vegetable garden, so if I'm stumped about something, I can look out the window and hopefully find the answer. I use caller ID and check e-mail only at specified times during the day. Like many working parents, I don't have time to waste time. Weekends and evenings, however, are for family and unless I have something pressing to finish, writing is out. The exception is when a brainstorm comes along. Then you need to write down your thoughts immediately, lest you forget them. Better to take the time to textualize your idea than to kick yourself later because you can't recall the idea.

When you've got a deadline, sometimes you have to write for hours at a time. This is when your accumulated good health and discipline can assist you. Since sitting in front of a computer all day holds no appeal whatsoever for me and would be physically impossible, I take breaks every hour or so by doing sit-ups or a bit of housework, or going for a run. One colleague once told me that to ward off headaches he takes a break from looking at his computer screen by using binoculars to look into the distance to find birds.

Equipment

If you're going to write, you must have the basic desk supplies. Pencils, pens, staples, and clips are obvious. I find that a computer is integral, although some writers avoid them out of intimidation. My major professor refused to purchase a computer and typed all of his thirty-six books on a clunky old typewriter.

Computers are crucial for the Internet and e-mail access. Many sources for your project can be obtained on-line. A colleague of mine goes through two printers a year because she prints out so many essays from Web sites. Some writers have a fax machine to make it easier to send material back and forth to publishers and major professors.

On my desk is my water bottle and places for coffee mugs and soft drinks (and the occasional wine for later in the evening), cheery flowers, and remote control for the stereo and television. (I watch TV only when I'm writing a first draft.) In the top drawer of my filing cabinet are vitamins, chewing gum, aspirin, lip balm, lotion, candy, and other comforts.

You should acquire an arsenal of editing books to help you. For the classes I have taught that included writing components, both nonfiction and fiction, I suggested to my students that they purchase the most recent editions of Stephen Manhard's *Goof-Proofer: How to Avoid the 41 Most Embarrassing Errors in Your Speaking and Writing* (New York: Collier Books, 1998); Arthur Plotnik's *Elements of Editing* (New York: Macmillan, 1996); Margaret Shertzer's *Elements of Grammar* (New York: Longman, 1996); William Strunk Jr. and E. B. White's *Elements of Style* (New York: Pearson Higher Education, 2000); and Kate Turabian's *Manual for Writers of Term Papers, Theses, and Dissertations* (Chicago: University of Chicago Press, 1996).

Staying Focused

Many writers stray from their topic and write about all kinds of peripheral issues, otherwise known as "going off on a tangent." One way to stay focused is to write the title of your work, essay, or chapter on a yellow self-adhesive note and put that below your computer screen so you can easily see it. Make sure that everything you write relates directly to that topic.

You may have a complicated plot or topic. Many scholars who take an interdisciplinary approach to research and analysis are often overwhelmed with information from a variety of disciplines, which makes it difficult to stay focused on just one issue. Consider that you don't have to start writing on page 1 and keep writing until page 300. I have never written a nonfiction or fiction book or essay in order. I write the passages I feel like writing at the moment, even if they are in chapters 1, 6, and 11. If you have many separate issues in your book or essay, this is a good strategy because you can write according to your mood when you turn on the computer.

Writing Groups and Chat Rooms

Many writers belong to writers' groups where they can find support, information about how to write, upcoming conferences, and the newest "must have" books on the market. Members of writers' groups often make good friends and find the meetings satisfying social events. But the upside of these groups goes hand-in-hand with the downside: many participants spend so much time traveling to and from meetings, endlessly critiquing others' papers, and chatting on-line *about* writing that they have little time left *for* writing.

While writers' groups can indeed be helpful, writers must make certain that they don't spend all their time talking instead of writing. Some people are never satisfied with anything that others write, and you could spend years endlessly rewriting just trying to please your critics. And remember, the larger the group, the less time the others will have to spend helping you.

Also beware of on-line chat rooms that feature Native topics. Many people lurk on those Listservs and have nothing better to do than send endless e-mails that have no relation to writing. I joined a Native literature listserv a few years ago and became quickly dismayed at the hundreds of messages that poured in (for the two weeks I endured it) about cat food, imaginary Indian grandmothers, and thank-yous for previous messages. Don't get sucked into these dialogues because you may never reemerge.

Be Careful with E-Mail

Electronic mail has drastically changed the way we communicate. We can send messages in seconds and forward others with a simple click of the mouse. This convenience is also a liability, because unlike letters we might write longhand, or documents to be printed out as letters, e-mails may not be as carefully edited.

E-mail allows us to send attachments (documents) along with our messages. If you like to send your work this way, be very careful that you have appropriate virus screens installed on your computer. Hackers can send viruses to you via e-mail through an attachment. Be certain that you know who sent the e-mail to you and that it is safe. Otherwise, a virus might cause you to lose everything on your hard drive.

Tips on Jumpstarting

If you're stuck, uninspired, bored, or suffering from other symptoms of writer's block, try any or all of the below:

● Start at the beginning of your manuscript and read it with the intention of only correcting errors. I have never *not* been inspired to write more if I approach my project this way.

● Read something written by your favorite author.

● Watch a television show or movie.

● Talk to other writers at a conference.

● Go to the mall and realize how much time you are wasting. This will get you back home in a hurry.

● Go to a bookstore and take in the number of books on the shelves. This bit of reality that you, too, can write will also get you home quickly.

Save Your Work

All of us have either heard about or experienced the horror of losing our work because of a computer crash or a "corrupted" disk or, as I kept hearing in graduate school, because the only copy of a dissertation was left on the top of a car and the owner drove off. While the last one sounds unbelievable, just talk to stressed-out grad students on a deadline for graduation and they often find it hard to remember their name, much less to put their manuscript back in the vehicle. Many of us simply forget to back up our work on a regular basis.

One way to remember to back up your work on a disk or CD is to ask yourself how much time you want to spend remembering what you wrote and retyping. If you don't want to recall a paragraph, then back up after each paragraph. Maybe you can recall an entire chapter or a page, but most of us cannot. It's up to you.

Q & A

Q: *I have no energy or enthusiasm for writing.*

A: Provided that you are a writer or student and must write (and not just someone who likes the idea of being a writer but does not want to go to the trouble of actually writing), then understand that most writers at some time or another become bored and want to move on to another topic or to quit altogether. Often what is needed is a mental reworking. Try and think of writing as fun. Even if you feel like you have nothing to say, write down something anyway. It may be drivel, but you don't have to use it and that bit of writing may jumpstart you.

Think of editing as a challenge. A Texas writer of ghost stories once said that she truly enjoys seeing how many unneeded words she can omit while editing. Of course, if you have a serious deadline, writing may seem like your enemy and stressful work. If this is the case, keep in mind that many writers do their best writing under the pressure of deadlines. If you keep telling yourself that, then maybe you can, too.

Q: *I am a Native student and am overwhelmed with having to deal with tribal issues and at the same time meeting the standards of the university. I simply have no inspiration to write.*

A: Native students often have to try to balance a variety of issues, not the least of which are racism, cultural differences, and lack of familial support. You, as a Native writer, have certain issues you must deal with: a job, your family, tax preparation, health care, and so on, just like most other people. But at the same time you also must tend to your responsibilities as a tribal member, which means you participate in ceremonies and try to meet your tribe's expectations of your doing work that will help the tribe. (Ironically, many of the same tribal people who encouraged you to get a degree may later criticize you for trying to be "better than everyone else.")

Through the years I have taught and mentored members of the Navajo, Hopi, Apache, Cherokee, Choctaw, Nez Perce, Dakota, Ho Chunk, Tohono O'Odham, Comanche, and Pawnee nations and tribes. The students who are the most "fired up" about writing (and this includes myself as a Choctaw woman) are those who are determined to help their tribes. They find topics that affect and interest them personally, such as economic development, pollution from uranium tailings, psychological problems resulting from colonialism, depression, language program development, sustainable energy development, ethnic fraud, treaty abrogation, spousal abuse, and racism in textbooks, as well as larger "umbrella" issues such as decolonization, nation-building, and empowerment. Students who begin to learn about how they can assist tribes in these areas become energized and enthusiastic. I have heard many of them say after lectures about avoiding complacency and getting involved, "That talk changed my life." I strongly urge Natives who are having problems in school, especially emotional ones, to start looking at how other Indigenous people are making a difference. There is nothing like a focus in life to get you motivated to work and write.

Q: *My major professor doesn't require me to contact the tribe I am writing about for my dissertation. And he never talked with Indians for any of the works he has written. Should I?*

A: This is an ethical and moral issue, not just for academics but also for nonacademic writers who focus on Natives as the subjects of their writing projects. You either have manners or you don't. You either gather information from all sources or you don't. Most times, no one can punish you for not being ethical or for not doing proper research, but be warned that tribes are being more aggressive about protecting themselves. The Hopis have declared disrespectful writers personae non grata on the reservation; the Havasupais have filed two multimillion-dollar suits against Arizona State University because of deceptive research conducted on tribal members; and across the country tribal members are publicly identifying unethical researchers. If you decide to take the easy way out, it's up to you figure out how to live with yourself.

CHAPTER FOUR

Writing Nonfiction

Nonfiction is just that: true stories and writings about Natives, past and present. There are many genres of nonfiction, some of which are included below.

Ethnographies

Ethnographers record the life stories told to them by others. Ethnography surged as a field in the 1920s as part of the Indian Reorganization Act in an attempt to help tribes recover knowledge and to retain what knowledge they had.

CHALLENGES OF WRITING ETHNOGRAPHIES

If the author is an observer of a culture but not a member of that culture and does not know the language or intricate cultural mores, then how can the reader be certain that what that author has written is true? Many times the listener misunderstands and incorrectly translates what the speaker says. Sometimes the writer purposely changes the narrator's voice to make a point. For example, according to people who know Mary Crow Dog, editor Richard Erdoes (a white male anthropologist) altered her speaking style in his *Lakota Woman* (New York: Harper, 1991) and rendered her unique voice almost unrecognizable.

Another example is a newspaper article on my husband's grandfather, Joshua Mihesuah, which was published in 1935 in the *Duncan Weekly Eagle*. Joshua and his wife, Carrie, were educated Comanches who had been forced to attend Fort Sill Boarding School in Oklahoma as children. The reporter asked Joshua about his experiences as a farmer, and instead of giving Joshua's literal response in clear, grammatical English, he wrote: "Me walk and push plow and cultivator. Learn how to raise corn. Am farmer now – raise crops and live good. Me farmer, you printer. . . . White men try to buy farm. No sell.

All mine. Raise crops, live good. No can do anything else. Just farm."
Needless to say, the family was humiliated by this distortion of Joshua's
speaking style, which misled hundreds of readers and gave the impression that he was an ignorant Comanche.

Many ethnographers misinterpret what Natives tell them. This is
a problem especially when the ethnographer uses a translator. Paula
Gunn Allen has written a terrific essay, "Kochinnenako in Academe:
Three Approaches to Interpreting a Keres Indian Tale" (in *The Sacred
Hoop: Recovering the Feminine in American Indian Traditions* [Boston:
Beacon Press, 1986]), that tells a traditional story about the change of
seasons. But outsiders (a male, a lesbian, and a traditional member
of the tribe) who listen to the story interpret it in a variety of ways
depending on their personal values and on what they want the story
to say about women and tribal values. This essay illustrates how listeners can misinterpret the significance and meaning of tribal stories
depending on their cultural background, expectations, and personal
bias.

Another challenge is that because writers of ethnographies must engage with Natives, they also must adhere to the tribe's research guidelines. And if they are scholars (and most ethnographers are scholars), they also must follow their institutional research guidelines. Many
writers are loath to go through this process and because there are
few schools that actually punish those who avoid this important step,
writers often do not bother to turn in their research proposals to IRB
committees.

Biographies and Memoirs

Biographies are life stories. The difference between biographies and
ethnographies is that biographers often write the life story of a person without his/her (or the family's and descendants') permission and
without talking to him/her to get information. Countless stories about
Sitting Bull, Geronimo, Black Hawk, and others have been written
without any input from members of their tribes, much less from their
descendants. I have researched the life of murdered American Indian
Movement activist Anna Mae Pictou-Aquash, but only after talking to
her family members to get their permission to write about her.

Many people have collections of letters and diaries of their lives to supplement their memories. A memoir might also be called an autobiography. Publishers are especially interested in using autobiographies of famous people. Not-so-famous folks often type their life stories and distribute them to friends and family members.

CHALLENGES OF WRITING BIOGRAPHIES AND MEMOIRS

The challenges of writing biographies are similar to those of writing histories: You may not acquire all the information you need without talking to the subject of your research. And if you do write your work, you may incur the wrath of the person – or that person's family – whom you did not talk to.

Most people can recall in vivid detail many events of their lives, but no one can remember everything. Gaps riddle our memories. Nor do people recall past events with complete accuracy. Wishful thinking, embellishment, and interferences from others – often family members with selective memories who try to fill in those gaps – can alter the stories.

History

Writing history requires that the writer investigate both oral testimonies and textualized data in order to create stories about what may have happened in the past. In traditional tribal cultures, young Natives are taught their histories so that they can use traditional knowledge to solve modern problems. Scholarly history will be heavily footnoted, and it often focuses on a specific person, event, or time period. Popular history is often written in a creative nonfiction style in order to appeal to a mainstream, not academic, audience. Popular history does not use academic jargon or theories and is often more "sweeping," covering spans of time and many people and usually cites only major sources.

CHALLENGES OF WRITING HISTORY

Although stories about historical events and people are supposed to be true, if the author did not live during the time period he/she is writing about, then how do we know the stories are correct? Natives have listened to stories for centuries, and it is part of their tradition to listen and learn from what they hear. Whether or not these stories are literally true cannot be ascertained by Western means. But that is not the point. Many Natives believe them; they have told stories for thousands of years before whites arrived in the Western Hemisphere. Their custom of passing down histories through oral tradition must be respected, and their stories should be used alongside textualized data.

Some people are not happy with revisionist historians – writers who take a look at the current interpretations of a past event and rewrite the nature of that event. In the past decade, Native revisionists have rewritten certain events in the history of Indian – white relations that put Native perspectives at the forefront instead of the voices of the victors. Traditional historians, however, believe that outsiders are the best ones to document tribal histories because Natives are too emotionally involved in the topic and cannot be objective. Conversely, Natives argue that outsiders cannot be objective because their biased opinions color their writings.

Textbooks

Texts are required reading for students. They are supposed give succinct information about a subject in a highly organized, easy-to-read, and understandable format.

CHALLENGES OF WRITING TEXTBOOKS

Textbooks have the potential to influence thousands of people. Texts are written in a particular format approved by the publisher and they must include an enormous amount of information in relatively few pages. And they must be thorough. If a textbook on American history does not discuss women, for example, then students might assume women were not important enough throughout American history to merit mention. The same is true of Natives and other underrepresented groups. Another challenge is developing patience and perseverance. A properly constructed textbook on American Indian history from contact to the present, for example, could take a decade to compile. This is why we don't see many of them. The same rationale goes for textbooks on Native women: the topic is too enormous and complex for most people to think seriously about tackling it.

Current Events

This type of writing focuses on events and issues of the moment. Under this heading are investigative journalism and the exploration of topics that might include biography and ethnography. Also included are political science and justice studies, two growing areas that focus on American Indian treaty law, treaty abrogation, juvenile justice studies, and much more.

CHALLENGES OF WRITING ABOUT CURRENT EVENTS

Investigative reporting can be among the most exciting and interesting of all writings. But there are few books of this type dealing with Natives, and most investigative reporting is in the form of newspaper articles and editorials.

Writers must take into consideration all sides of the story when writing about current events. If you plan on writing about a specific event or person, make certain that you do not generalize. Journalists, reporters, and editorial writers are supposed to give "just the facts, ma'am," although journalists in many publications, such as some religious papers, sneak in political views and biased statements to make a statement that the paper supports.

Political scientists must have a grasp of history, including the European intellectual trends that were influential in creating ideologies and policies that were (and still are) applied to the colonized Native peoples. Their challenge is to discuss the foundations of treaty law and how Natives are treated by the courts today in the face of a discipline that tends to ignore traditional tribal political traditions. Some of the best books in this area are Taiaiake Alfred's *Peace, Power, Righteousness: An Indigenous Manifesto* (Oxford University Press, 1999) and Robert A. Williams Jr.'s *American Indian in Western Legal Thought: The Discourses of Conquest* (Oxford University Press, 1993).

An example of how investigative reporting directly affects readers is that after September 11, although most of the country grieved for those lost in the terrorist attacks, many Natives had a different reaction. In my classes, where I have 90 to 100 percent Natives enrolled, my question about how they felt about the attacks got me a classroom of shrugs. Many students were upset by the brutality of the attack, but they also put the murders into a context that they could understand: Their people have suffered centuries of deception, murder, racism, and forced education at the hands of the American government; one student said that "America had it coming." While this may seem a tough attitude, it is the viewpoint of many Natives and cannot be ignored. Although some Natives may appear to be flag-waving patriots, many more are not.

Another prominent current issue surrounds Lori Piestewa, the young Hopi mother and U.S. soldier who died during an incursion into Iraq. She has been heralded as a heroine, and the Arizona legislature has been pressured to rename Squaw Peak and Squaw Peak Parkway to Piestewa Peak and Piestewa Parkway, even though Arizona law dictates that five years must elapse after a person's death before renaming a geographical feature or roadway in someone's honor. While no one disputes the tragedy of her death, many Natives have grown weary of what they view as a colonialistic ploy. Thousands of women have perished defending their lands in the five-hundred-plus years since contact, yet they have never received this kind of attention. Why Piestewa? Although she is the first Native woman to die "in combat," the distinction must be made as to what kind of combat. Combat in which Natives fight against U.S. the Oppressor? Or combat in which Natives fight with U.S. the Oppressor?

Some books that discuss current events in Indian Country are M. Annette Jaimes, *The State of Native America: Genocide, Colonization and Resistance* (Cambridge MA: South End Press, 1992); Winona LaDuke, *All Our Relations: Native Struggles for Land and Life* (Cambridge MA: South End Press, 1999); and Jack Utter, *American Indians: Answers to Today's Questions* (Lake Ann MI: National Woodlands Publishing Company, 1993).

Most tribes have their own tribal newspapers; check individual Web sites. Good sources of current information about tribal events include
Indian Country Today at http://www.indiancountry.com
Native American Times at http://www.nativetimes.com
News from Indian Country at
http://www.indiancountrynews.com/index.cfm

Social Sciences

There are numerous fields under this heading, including social work and psychology, and many more subfields connected to them. Researchers must deal with real people but they often use statistics to obtain conclusions.

CHALLENGES OF WRITING IN THE SOCIAL SCIENCES

Natives often complain that a major obstacle to writing is that the status quo is not amenable to their research and writing that applies directly to Native communities. They also face the challenge of having to acknowledge Western theories and ways of healing (so readers will know they are informed) in addition to incorporating those aspects of healing that are more pertinent to Native communities: the psyche, spirituality, emotions, culture, and responsibility to the community.

Columns

Columns are often opinion pieces on a specific, timely topic. Columns usually must be a certain number of words and often must be written in a short period of time with a strict deadline. Columnists who write about Native issues chose short topics that are of interest to a wide audience.

CHALLENGES OF WRITING COLUMNS

Columns must be short, concise, entertaining, and informative. You have to get going in the first sentence and not have a long introduction. You must work fast and be able to edit quickly to get the work in on time.

"Train of Thought" Works and Self-Discovery Papers

"Train of thought" (TOT) works contain thoughts that are written down as they occur. Self-discovery (SD) works focus entirely on the author and his/her desire to come to grips with an event or psychological issue. Many of these concern travels through a reservation, interaction with a Native, or a desire to find one's ancestry.

CHALLENGES OF WRITING TOT WORKS AND SD PAPERS

The problem with TOT works is that they often are disorganized. TOT papers are usually one- or two-page paragraphs, have long sentences, and have no interconnectedness between the paragraphs. There often is no research associated with these kinds of works. Unless the author is familiar with the topic he/she is writing about and is a good, organized writer, TOT works are best left for diaries and letters to friends or family who can tolerate them.

The challenges associated with SD papers are similar to those of TOT works because they also are not organized. If there is any research, it is used selectively to support the thesis of the writer. I receive one SD paper each month at the *AIQ* office, which invariably involves the writer's quest to prove that he/she is part Indian.

Conference Papers

Writing and delivering conference papers is a major component of academic life. Many scholars are required to present papers at conferences in order to receive promotion and tenure, and delivering papers is an effective way for people to get to know your work. Papers delivered at scholarly conferences are supposed to fit a particular theme, along with the other three or four presentations. Each presenter gives a fifteen- to twenty-minute talk. Afterward a "commenter" gives a summary presentation, then the audience asks questions.

CHALLENGES OF WRITING CONFERENCE PAPERS

Presenters must stick to the time limit (although many listeners are more impressed if you finish prior to the deadline), which means you must stringently organize your paper and pay close attention to editing. Reading your paper out loud prior to the presentation is a must, although this does not ensure that you have anticipated all questions from the audience. You also should not send a conference *paper* to a journal without first revising it into a scholarly *article*. Many conference papers are written hastily and come across more like ideas spoken out loud than work that has been carefully considered and edited. Worse, many conference commenters lament that they did not receive the presenters' papers until the night before (instead of the requisite one month before the conference). How can they possibly be expected to deliver a decent summary? They can't, which is why many established scholars won't accept invitations to serve as "session commenter."

Book Reviews

Reviews are critiques of books and, like conference papers, academics are expected to do them. They are not supposed to be book reports like we wrote in high school. Publishers already tell us what books are about; reviews tell us whether those books are worth reading, have the correct information, and are written well. Reviews are what readers look at in order to decide whether they want to read a certain book. Reviews are also useful in succinctly summarizing the book's theme.

CHALLENGES OF WRITING BOOK REVIEWS

Many reviews end up being more like reports instead of telling us if the book does what it is supposed to. A good review should tell us about the author and briefly discuss the thesis. It should then give a critique of its accuracy, author bias, and writing style and then compare it to others on the same topic.

Anthologies

An anthology is a collection of essays focusing on a common theme written by a group of authors or a group of previously published essays written by one author. Anthologies can also consist of short stories, personal essays, and biographies.

CHALLENGES OF EDITING ANTHOLOGIES

Any editor of an anthology can tell you that compiling a group of papers from a variety of people is not as easy as it may seem. Not only must the editor compose a logical and compelling rationale for the book, he/she must then decide whom to invite to contribute. Then he/she must do the inviting and usually has to make the invitation attractive, which means having a publisher who wants the book so the "big names" will agree to participate in the project. So, backtrack a bit and make sure that you've contacted an interested publisher who will tell you in writing that they may consider the thing if you get the "big names." You must make certain that the contributors know exactly what they are to write about and that they cannot go off onto their own tangents. Some will do this anyway and it's up to you to make certain that they follow instructions. Sometimes it takes much work to get your writers to cooperate.

The other challenges to editing an anthology are rather large and tricky. First, you often have to hound your contributors to get the papers in by the deadline. It is annoying for the writers who get their papers in to you quickly to be told that the project is delayed because the other contributors are late. Another hurdle to overcome is dealing with contributors who don't come through at all. For example, the "distinguished" anthropologist invited to write an essay on women for my special issue in *AIQ*'s 1996 "Writing about (Writing about) American Indians" (that later became *Natives and Academics: Researching and Writing about American Indians* [Nebraska, 1998]) never sent in her paper, nor would she respond to certified letters asking her to tell me if she planned to honor her commitment. Her behavior was perplexing considering that she demanded a list of the other participants before committing to the project – which she did. So, I wrote an essay ("Commonalty of Difference: American Indian Women in History") myself in less than a week in order to meet the deadline. Two graduate students, a Navajo woman and Hopi man in the history department at Northern Arizona University NAU did not come through with their coauthored piece either, despite repeated promises. Sometimes you have to do without. In the latter case, the special issue was better for the omission, but this is not always the case. Sometimes the best writers disappoint you.

Another challenge is that some of the essays that do come in are inadequate. Although you can assist the author in revising, oftentimes the piece is hopeless and you have to let it go regardless of who the author is. For *Indigenizing the Academy*, my coeditor (Waziyatawiŋ Angela Wilson) and I had to turn down a piece from a prominent Indigenous activist because she did not – and would not – follow directions. She was furious that we rejected her paper, and though we were disappointed in her prima donna attitude, it simply cannot be our worry. Nor should it be yours if you have to do something similar.

Ask one or two more authors to write for you at the onset knowing that you will lose one or two by the end of the project.

Some anthologies are compilations of papers presented at a conference. These collections might appear to be somewhat easier to deal with because the authors and topics are set. Often, all that is needed is a revision of the papers so that they conform to the standards of the publisher. But getting the authors to make those revisions is the serious challenge.

You as editor also must make certain that all the papers conform to the theme of the book. I have been presented with too many special issues for *AIQ* and the Contemporary Indigenous Issues series that are supposed to be anthologies, but they really are groups of mismatched papers. Those that don't fit with the theme stick out like red flags. It is not easy to edit an anthology and sometimes it may prove easier to get the coherence you need by writing the entire book yourself.

What You Have to Do

So what kind of nonfiction writing will you do? Regardless of which you choose, there are a few things to keep in mind.

KEEPING THE READERS INTERESTED

A major challenge in writing is to keep your readers wanting to turn the page. Most theses and dissertations, for example, are not particularly compelling because they are degree requirements meant to demonstrate your ability to cite relevant literature in your area of study, your skill at being a library rat, your talent of organizing your notes and thoughts, and your skill at textualizing the results of your research. Dissertations include extraordinarily long acknowledgments (Mom, Dad, and all other relatives and friends are often mentioned) and bibliographies that include works not mentioned in the text. Your major professor is required to read it and occasionally another researcher will read the finished product if you have an original topic. Not many others look at it, however. And with good reason. Most dissertations are intense and boring (and often intensely boring) because as opposed to a book manuscript, the student writer's project includes the most basic information that readers are familiar with. Dissertations rarely contain cutting-edge ideas mainly because student writers are afraid to shock the dissertation committee. Once free of degree-requirement restraints, the new professor then hopefully sets out for more research and much rewriting in order to lose the "dissertationeze," that is, the elementary language and tedious "common knowledge" explanations.

Much of that rewriting entails adding elements that make your book interesting. Even if we know the outcome of your work, such as the allotment period in Indian Territory, the Cherokee Trail of Tears, or Custer's Last Stand, it is up to you to make the work appealing and unique. A good work that exemplifies creative nonfiction is Evan S. Connell's *Son of the Morning Star* (North Point Press, 1997), which deals with Custer's life and death.

There are hundreds of books and more essays written about Custer. Why so many? Everyone has access to the same textualized source material, but they have different perceptions about what they read and what they hear from informers. Custer fan clubs are in enthusiastic operation throughout the world. As with the immensely popular topic of the Civil War, some events and people inspire rage, admiration, a desire to know more, or a desire to see their image vanquished forever. What are some elements that will make your work one that readers will want to stay with to the end?

EMOTIONS

What do the individuals think as they endure their ordeals? Are they nervous, stressed, angry? How do you suppose Natives felt as they watched their land disappear, their loved ones die, and their culture alter and diminish? What about the children forced to attend boarding schools? How did their parents feel? What went through the minds of the soldiers who closed in on tribes and opened fire? What sorts of emotions allow a soldier to kill a child?

MOTIVATIONS

What motivated the individuals in your story to act the way they did? Custer wanted to be president some day, and he thought that being an "Indian fighter" in the same vein as Washington, Harrison, and Jackson would garner him support. A desire for power can be as strong as religious fervor.

HEALTH OF THE PLAYERS

What was the health – both mental and physical – of your players? Otto L. Bettmann's book, *The Good Old Days – They Were Terrible!* (Random House, 1974), discusses in graphic detail the everyday health problems Americans faced throughout history. What were the sanitation conditions of the setting in your story? What was the life span of the people? Medical care may be adequate today, but only in the last one hundred years has anesthesia been available. How did people deal with gunshots? Stabbings? Tooth cavities? Migraines? Appendicitis?

RELATIONSHIPS

What were the gender roles of those you write about? Traditionally, gender roles were quite specific among tribes. What were the prevailing views about gender in white society? How white men viewed women often dictated how they viewed and dealt with Natives. What about homosexuality? Discipline of children?

Topics Natives Would Like You to Consider

It is fairly obvious that the problems faced by Natives today are a direct result of colonization, and the repercussions are still felt today. Natives who deal with empowerment issues talk about "internalized colonization." Because tribes were changed drastically after contact and they are still colonized, all of these topics – along with how tribes deal with these issues today – are open for more discussion:

● Loss of land
● Loss of population (many Natives refer to the dramatic population loss as a "holocaust")
● Dependence on material goods brought by the invaders
● Unprecedented intertribal fighting because of competition for material goods
● Influx of Christianity
● Intertribal factionalism
● Destruction of gender roles
● Extreme psychological stress
● Alcoholism and other forms of self-abuse

● Physiological change brought about by intermarriage with non-Natives

● Practical solutions backed up by data that can assist tribes in solving their myriad problems such as poverty, racism, discrimination, alcoholism, and depression, in addition to suggestions for better environmental management, economic development, nation-building, decolonization, and empowerment

● Information about "boarding school syndrome." We already have scads of books and essays on boarding schools. What we need to investigate now is the impact of forced education on the psychology of succeeding generations.

Because the effects of colonization have persisted through the years, all of these topics and those related to them can be investigated by educators, historians, anthropologists, psychologists, social workers, political scientists, philosophers, and religious scholars, as well as those who are not academically trained. In other words, these are topics that cut across disciplines and socioeconomic classes. They are fair game for any writer. An indispensable guide for writers interested in tackling tribal issues head-on is Linda Tuhiwai Smith's *Decolonizing Methodologies: Research and Indigenous Peoples* (New York: St. Martin's Press, 1999).

CHAPTER FIVE

Writing Fiction

Most of American Indian "fiction" is based on fact. Native writers who have lived close to their culture have a plethora of stories and emotions to draw from. They can recount tribal stories and history from the tribal perspective, not to mention firsthand encounters with the effects of colonization: racism, prejudice, self-hatred, poverty, forced education, violence, alcoholism, loss of culture, and the subjugation of women. They also know about survival, happiness, hope, and determination from the point of view of people who live this way. From a Native perspective, plots are not difficult to come by.

Challenges of Writing Fiction

Natives often have a worldview formed by living among other tribal peoples that is not the same as that of mainstream America. Native cultures are also distinct from one another. Clans and individuals within those cultures, in turn, are vastly diverse and it is hard, if not impossible, for outsiders to understand those differences. If you have not lived these experiences, it does not mean you can't try to write about them. But why would you?

On a related note, there are many books written by Natives who have only recently discovered their heritage or who are not even sure of their heritage. Those books are also questionable sources of information about what Native life is really like. Some fiction writers want to write their poems, novels, and stories without being accountable for accuracy. Some believe they should be able to use tribal languages in any manner they wish, without checking with fluent readers to see if their words and phrases are correct. This lack of desire to be accountable (and ethical) is a serious issue in the field of American Indian literary criticism today.

There are plenty of books about Indians written by non-Indians.

The late Asa Carter (d. 1979), the author of the immensely popular *Education of Little Tree*, the "autobiography" of a Cherokee orphan, had claimed to be Cherokee and his book shot to the top of the *New York Times* best-seller list. His use of the Cherokee language was incorrect and Native readers knew immediately that his references to Cherokee culture were cultivated from secondary sources (books). He was exposed as a fraud, a white man who was a member of the Ku Klux Klan, in fact. It didn't seem to matter to non-Natives, who still bought his novel in droves.

Many authors forge ahead and write about tribes and are popular among white Americans who also don't know any better. There are more than enough books that tell us about "Indians and animals" or an "Indian boy and his wise grandfather." If you aren't familiar with tribal cultures, then tackling a Native topic and churning out an inferior work may not only be embarrassing, you may find yourself ostracized and boycotted by the very people you are writing about.

A prime example of how fiction can be stranger than truth and much more damaging is the aforementioned *Hanta Yo* (1979) by Ruth Beebe Hill, an "epic" novel that purports to be an authentic look at Lakota life and culture. The tribe was horrified by Hill's explicit sexual descriptions, and no less than the Black Hills Claims and Treaties Council in South Dakota condemned the book and tried to block the television version of the story. Numerous Native intellectuals wrote about the book's inaccuracies. Hill reacted by telling the Natives who opposed her work that she knew more about them than they did themselves. Sadly, the television miniseries aired and millions of Americans who knew nothing about tribes then received many hours of miseducation.

The field of American Indian literature is vast and complex. Most of the scholars who specialize in "American Indian Literature" do not write. They analyze the work others have written. On the one hand, Native writers of fiction are looked upon by many non-Natives (and naive Natives) as the "experts" of Native history and culture and as spokespeople for tribal America. On the other hand, they are also seen by many Native activists as writers who have escaped to a field of study where they can claim Indianness without having their claims checked and where they can write any scenario without bothering to check the facts about their tribe's history and culture. While many mainstream novels about Natives often do not tell us enough about the characters, Native stories often tell us too much. An overdose of the same kind of character angst about being mixed-blood, poverty-stricken, depressed, and so on is tedious and uninspiring. Finding a useful and truthful balance to imaginary scenarios is the great challenge to Native fiction writers.

Types of Fiction Works

CHILDREN'S STORIES AND BOOKS

I put this heading in the fiction arena because the majority of books I have read aimed at young audiences come across as fiction, even if they are meant to be nonfiction. Perhaps it is because the majority of "Indian stories" for kids are written by authors who don't know much if anything about tribal cultures. Children are impressionable, and children's books can make a tremendous impact on their lives. Children believe what they read, see, and hear, and if they are exposed to stereotypical literature, they will believe it unless intervention takes place.

Tribal stories serve several purposes. According to the Dakota historian Waziyatawiŋ Angela Wilson, stories are told in order to solidify the listener's connection to land and place, to celebrate and transmit culture "upon which our survival as a people depends," to declare our resiliency, and to teach. They are not for mere entertainment and should not be treated as such.

Most children's literature about Indians centers on the same themes: a child and his/her wise grandfather; a child and his/her animal friend; a child and his/her experience with the supernatural, usually involving a talking animal. The problem is that most of these stories are told by non-Natives with little knowledge about tribal realities and less understanding about the meaning of tribal stories that are termed "myths" by non-Indians. Most of these non-Native authored books that exploit tribal culture are written for profit. They are not meant to educate anyone, especially not Natives who already know this information.

Like most parents, I am concerned about what my children read. But as a Native parent, I must make certain that my kids read stories that are truthful about Native history and culture, not fabricated, mystical, or "feel-good," or, worse, talk about our ancestors in negative terms. I have been more than a little shocked on several occasions to hear from my young children that their teacher or classmates said that "all Indians are dead" or that my son isn't really an Indian because he doesn't wear braids.

The problem with children's literature that includes Natives is multifold. Cornel Pewewardy, a Kiowa/Comanche educator, terms this problem with stereotyping the "Pocahontas Paradox" because Pocahontas was a real individual and many Americans want to understand her and other Natives, but they continue to use stereotypes and fabricated images in order to comprehend them. Many of the stereotypes mentioned in chapter 2 do indeed pervade children's literature, but here are some specific issues to consider if you plan on writing Native literature for children:

● Keep in mind that books last a long time and generations of children will be influenced by your work.

● If you plan on using prominent tribal stories (some people call them "legends"), do not change them to suit your purposes. Stories are used to teach lessons to tribal members and it is not up to writers to change them to make them more interesting so the author can make money. Do not combine stories from several tribes to make a separate story in order to make a point or to make the tale more interesting. Tribal stories are intricate and have a real purpose.

● Similarly, do not trivialize the spirituality of tribes, as Paul Gobel has done with the complex, sophisticated stories of the Sioux. "Coyote," "sweat lodge," "sun dance," "peyote," and "powwow" are terms that cut across many tribal cultures. They encompass many images, philosophies, and religious meanings. If you do not understand them, do not use them.

● Tribes have oral traditions. That is, communications were transmitted by word of mouth. Some stories are not meant to be textualized. What may sound like a great, marketable story might not work as well on paper because the story is meant to be told orally only.

● If you're using dialogue, don't make the characters sound like ignoramuses. Using phrases like "heap big buffalo" or "me happy to see White Eyes, my Brother!" makes Natives appear stupid. If you use them, we can say the same about you.

65

• Illustrators must know what they are drawing. If you are telling a Comanche story, the illustrator must not use Arizona landscaping. A story about an Oklahoma Choctaw should not be enhanced by drawings of tipis and headdresses. Because many tribes (Navajo, Cherokee, Choctaw, Plains, and Iroquois, for example) believe owls are messengers of bad omens, including death, it is inappropriate to create an illustration of a Native person with an owl on his/her arm or shoulder.

• Don't go overboard in your descriptions. If a Native character is outdoors, there is no reason to have that person commune with every butterfly and flower.

• Picture books are usually short, and because only a few images can be used, authors tend to use photographs of historic Natives, not those in the present. Children need to be made aware that Natives are not only alive today, they rarely dress as their ancestors did.

• Create a realistic title. If you're writing about an Indian child in New York, there is no reason to call it "Scared Little Black Fox and His Big City Adventure." Many people would be scared to visit New York, but Indians are often made to appear as if they in particular are too unsophisticated and backward to deal with city life or school or the dentist.

• Using the subtitle "An American Indian Story/Legend/Myth" may be catchy, as is the bold sentence that the author is of "Indian or _____ [fill in tribe] descent," but if you use these phrases, you better make certain they are absolutely true. The same can be said of the informer you use to get the story in the first place.

• Many Natives are angry that many non-Native authors of children's books become "experts" on Native history and culture and are frequently asked to speak in schools on topics they know very little about. You may want to do some soul searching before embarking on such a venture.

• Do not tell a story about the past without also telling about the present. While this may rankle some who believe they should be able to tell a historic story in a vacuum, the problem in the realm of children's literature is that children *already believe* that Natives only lived in the past. Don't contribute to the stereotype.

• Make certain that you thoroughly identify who you are writing about. Caldecott Medal winner Gerald McDermott, in his *Arrow to the Sun: A*

Pueblo Indian Tale (Puffin Books, 1977), doesn't bother to tell us which of the eighteen Pueblo tribes he is writing about. Pueblos, for sure, have not only been dismayed to see in print a generic – and incorrect – discussion of a kiva (a sacred structure where Hopis worship and conduct ceremonies), they are just as angry that such a generic story won the prestigious book award, an endorsement that tells the world this is an accurate story. And it is not.

For more information about stereotypes in children's literature, see Arlene Hirschfelder, Paulette Fairbanks Molin, and Yvonne Wakin, *American Indian Stereotypes in the World of Children: A Reader and Bibliography* (Landham MD: Rowman and Littlefield, 1999); Beverly Slapin and Doris Seale, *Through Indian Eyes: The Native Experience in Books for Children* (Los Angeles: American Indian Studies Center, UCLA, 1998); Naomi Caldwell-Wood and Lisa A. Mitten, *Selective Bibliography and Guide for "I" Is Not for Indian: The Portrayal of Native Americans in Books for Young People* (Program of the ALA/OLOS Subcommittee for Library Services to American Indian People, American Indian Library Association, 1991) at http://www.nativeculture.com/lisamitten/ailabib. htm.

Also useful is Karen D. Harvey, Lisa D. Harjo, and Lynda Welborn, *How to Teach about American Indians: A Guide for the School Library Media Specialist* (Landham MD: Scarecrow, 1999).

ROMANCE NOVELS

One bookstore staple is the romance novel section. Romance is a multi-million-dollar industry – and that can be for just one author. When a Native character is used, it's usually the male who looks Native, but ultimately that person turns out to be a white man who was adopted by an Indian family as a baby, tans well, and is really the offspring of wealthy parents. This satisfies the requirement that interracial love affairs be approached very carefully, if at all, and it satisfies those who demand that the hero and heroine be of the same racial group. It is a deceptive way of having white female characters interact with an exotic "man of color" who really is not.

Another type of fiction work is a hybrid of fiction and personal accounts. My novel, *The Roads of My Relations*, chronicles eleven generations of a Choctaw family and is based almost entirely on the stories told to me by my family. The first chapter is based on the murder of my great-grandfather, who was a Choctaw merchant killed in the 1880 violence in Indian Territory at the hands of a gang of mixed-blood Choctaws and blacks who hatcheted him to death. This was a real occurrence and is documented in S. W. Harmon's *Hell on the Border* (Fort Smith AR: Phoenix, 1898). The very real history of the Choctaw Nation is in there, too, but the situations the family encounters are fabricated by me. My other fiction is based on my realities, such as my years in competitive athletics, search and rescue, and sled-dog racing, but underpinning it all is the reality of the tribe. If you are writing a fiction story based on true events, the ethical thing to do is properly credit the source of your ideas: a newspaper article, a book, or the work of another writer. Any less is akin to plagiarism.

Where Do Ideas Come from?

All writers, regardless of what they write about, must come up with ideas. I tell my students to carry small notebooks with them (in their purse, pocket, or briefcase) and to keep one by the side of their bed. I have several: one for my purse, one on my office desk at NAU, one on the bedside table, and a small one in the fanny pack I run with. Anytime you have an idea, write it down; the chances are great that you will not remember that bright idea or observation later. Do not think you can remember "priceless" quotes and sunset descriptions – you won't. Write thoughts down when they occur to you. Then, when you can't think of what to write or how to write it, go back and revisit what you have stashed in your notebooks.

For fiction writing, much of what I write is based on my realities, so I look through my photograph albums. If your high school annuals make you cringe, then you have a wealth of information about emotions, hairstyles, acne, and relationships just waiting for you to analyze!

When writing fiction, it is crucial to include details that bring your characters to life. What are the smells, sounds, sights, and tastes of the situation? What are some ways to find these details? Writing fiction can be wonderful therapy. Many writers find that the act of writing is a release and relief. How can you enhance the experience? Here are some ideas for creating interesting characters by reflecting on yourself and people you know well (most of these are aimed toward Native writers, although non-Native writers can also use them to create characters and situations):

● *How do you express yourself?* Is it through singing, dancing, painting, arguing, criticizing, remaining silent?

● *What interests you?* I ask my Native students what they would rather be doing than sitting in class. What music would they listen to? What books would they read? What movies would they watch? What is their ideal vacation spot? What makes them feel secure?

● *What do you know about?* If you're planning to write a story about life on a particular reservation, you had better know what it is like to live there – you need to be an actual resident. Otherwise, you come across as a know-it-all interloper out to make money like Ian Frazier in his insulting, problematic *On the Rez*.

● *What things did you like best when you were a child and what five things do you like best now?*

● *What makes you angry?* Why? How do you react physically when you are mad? Do you sweat, get a headache, throw up?

● *What are the most significant events in your life, both positive and negative?*

● *Observe people when you go to breakfast, lunch, or dinner in a public place.* What are they eating? What do they wear? Is someone flouncing her hair on a first date? Is someone picking his nose? How old are the people you see? What do you think they do for a living?

● *What can you recall about the places in which you lived?* What about climate, your house, plants and animals, streams, hills, and mountains? What were some major events in your life that you experienced at these spots? What events may have happened historically in these areas?

● *Chronicle one day in your life.* How do you feel physically throughout the day? What are the sights, sounds, smells, colors, and stresses that you encounter? Does time move fast or slow? What do you eat and why? Did you eat good or bad food? Did you encounter bad drivers?

● *What are your favorite foods?* Are they spicy or sweet? For example,

"I love the smooth, creamy texture of melted chocolate on ice cream. It reminds me of my first date with ⸻ where we ate from the same dish as we listened to Nirvana."

• *What are physical traits of people?* Eye color, scars, warts, hair length, fingernail polish, posture, speech patterns, physical problems, or physique. This list is endless.

• *What do you dislike?* Foods, bugs, clowns, rap music? What sensorial effects do these things have on you? What about psychological effects?

• *Use photographs from your life.* What do you recall about the time the pictures were taken? Colors, smells, place, people, what you did before and after the picture was taken, time period, songs you associate with the photo. What happened to the people, animals, building, and other objects, in the photo?

• *What are significant items in your home?* (This doesn't include the sink or toilet unless those items are special in some way.) Why did you choose these items? What do they say about you and/or the other people in the home?

The Above Exercises Do Help

Because of the sordid events I have encountered in academia, I have had a wealth of personal experience facing racism and sexism as a Native woman. And because I had lived it, I could write my novel, *Statement of Expectations*, the story of the murder of a Native anthropologist at the hands of racist, jealous anthropologists. Interestingly, although this novel is based on my real experiences with racism and prejudice in the academy, one reviewer called the story "wildly imaginative," which goes to show that the life experiences of Native writers and white reviewers are drastically different.

What to Do with Your Ideas

Now that you have plenty of interesting emotional, physical, and personality traits for your characters, along with sights, sounds, and tastes, you need to ask yourself some important questions:

• What is your plot?
• Who are your characters?

- How will the story move?
- What can readers learn from it?
- How is it original and unique?

Fiction Topics That Have Been Overdone

You can have great character traits and sensory development, but if you use the same old plots, then we don't care. Try and avoid these topics, unless they are incidental to the unique plot you hopefully can create:

- Mixed-blood confusion
- Alcoholism
- Poverty
- Spousal/child/self-abuse
- Sadness/despair/guilt
- Helplessness
- Stereotypes about witchcraft, shape-shifters, characters who talk to the cosmos, and so on

What We Need More of

Few readers (and movie watchers) can tolerate sustained discussions and descriptions about tragedy and heartbreak. As a Native historian who has to research this kind of thing for a living and who has seen and experienced plenty of it in my lifetime, I certainly don't turn to this genre for entertainment. Neither does anyone else I know. Try to create stories that contain these elements:

- Happiness
- Problem solving
- Viewpoints of traditional tribal members
- Determination
- Funny and bright characters who are optimistically trying to find ways to empower themselves and their Nations. These are called "role models."
- Characters who are able to interact with mainstream society and their tribe without breaking down emotionally

● Connection to land and tribal rights

If you can create an upbeat, truthful, humorous, and inspiring work about Native America, then your book will be useful and potentially successful.

Difficulties in Getting Published

The field of Native literary criticism is highly territorial and competitive. Fiction works written by Natives are scrutinized in terms of character identity and sexuality, the "purpose of" place and humor, ceremonies, names, and language usage. Many students of literary criticism purport to be experts on these topics, but Native writers have found again and again not only that the reviewers of most works are not even Native, they often possess limited knowledge and much ego about their "expertise" about the realities of tribal life. To make matters worse, many of the editors in charge of sending out these submitted books for review also are ignorant. In addition, only a handful of Native writers control the market, not only in terms of being the most popular writers (even though equally talented writers are out there but are being ignored), but only a few writers control the Native Literature lists of the few university presses that publish Native fiction. See more in chapter 9.

Q & A

Q: *Why is it that Natives object to works that utilize an "Indian informer"? And why do some Natives like a novel such as* Hanta Yo *while others do not?*

A: As I have written repeatedly, not all Natives are alike and there are several reasons why there might be differences of opinion over what is "good" or "bad." Some Natives know nothing about their culture because they either were adopted by non-Natives, were shamed into rejecting their culture, or are mainly white and never had access to their culture (these people often claim to be Native by virtue of blood, not cultural knowledge). Some Natives are well aware of their history and culture but are also eager to make a buck. They will give information to writers – whether or not it is really true – and they also will take cultural artifacts to sell to collectors. Authors may use Native informers, but they often are not at all representative of the rest of the tribe. Many writers will look for informers who will tell them exactly what they want to hear and because they are Native, the authors believe their work is legitimized.

CHAPTER SIX

Ethics in Research and Writing

Many nonfiction scholars writing about Natives know that if they plan on focusing on Indians, especially if they are writing about cultural issues such as religion, then they must secure permission from that tribe before trying to publish their work. If you (whether you're Native or non-Native) plan on writing about Hopis, for example, you should be prepared to be told by the tribe's Cultural Preservation Office (http://www.nau.edu/ hcpo-p) that your topic is not approved.

Why is this? Hopis have been victimized for decades by unscrupulous filmmakers and researchers who use sensitive tribal information (such as religious aspects) for their own benefit. Despite the tribe's attempts to ban cameras from their ceremonies, many people still sneak cameras, video cameras, and tape recorders into the villages. As a result, the Hopis have banned all non-Hopis from most of their ceremonies.

Weary of being written about in endless stereotypical and incorrect ways, many other tribes have also created their own research guidelines.

Conversing and Listening

If you are writing about Natives, you must talk to them. Traditionally, tribes passed their histories and stories verbally. Many Natives today still uphold those traditions and are well aware of their history and culture. A major controversy raging through Native Studies today is between non-Natives who believe they can adequately write about Natives without talking to them and Natives who are appalled that anyone can claim accuracy just by researching a tribe's history in the library. The issue is complex and volatile, and it is not the purpose of this book to discuss it in any depth. However, it is up to the author to take it upon him/herself not only to secure permission to write about sensitive/familial topics but also to talk to the tribal people themselves to get their perspectives on the issue.

Guidelines to Follow

In 1991 I chaired NAU's Native American Research Guidelines and Advisory Committee, a group of five scholars charged with researching the problem of knowledge appropriation and ethical transgressions when researching and writing about Indians and then creating guidelines to assist scholars who wish to write about tribes.

To give an indication of how controversial these types of guidelines are, consider that the university never instituted them because of pressure from powerful faculty who believed they could (and can) write about Indians in any way they want. Because even (white) members of the committee did not want to include too many guidelines that gave tribes power over what research can be conducted on them, I expanded the guidelines. Tribes believe they should be used and many tribes have in fact used these guidelines to create their own. As an author of Native topics you must read them and use them.

1. Only the tribes' elected political and religious leadership should review and approve the research proposal. Many writers believe that because they have talked with "an Indian" that this one voice is all they need to legitimize their work. As you have read repeatedly by now, not all Indians are alike, and each tribe has its own tribal political leadership and tribal religious leadership. Many Indians know absolutely nothing about their tribe's history or culture and have no business giving out information, much less granting permission to use that information.

2. Researchers should remain sensitive to the economic, social, physical, psychological, religious, and general welfare of the individuals and cultures being studied. Since contact, non-Natives have misunderstood Natives. The newcomers considered themselves to be "civilized," while the newly discovered Natives were seen as inferior and "uncivilized." This idea persists even today. If an outsider enters the world of another group, he/she usually is unaware of what constitutes proper behavior. Tribes do not care a whit if you're prolific or have won awards. You may even be seen as nosy and aggressive.

Many writers believe it's appropriate to take their observations of another culture and publish them. Quite simply, most Indians have no comprehension of why they are so darn interesting to outsiders. Some writers wonder why Natives refuse to protest a book if they don't like it. Simple: they would have to reveal the exact reasons why a book is offensive, thereby giving out information they don't want disseminated in the first place.

3. Researchers who are preparing grant applications that deal with Indians should be prepared to wait months, if not a year, for the subjects to thoroughly understand every aspect of the study. Don't pick a topic dealing with a tribe that has a track record of turning down requests for interviews, filming, and so on. If you apply to the Hopi tribe, for example, unless you have good friend at Hopi who can move your request along and are doing truly useful research, don't expect a positive answer – if at all. If you need a tribe's permission in time for a grant application or a publication deadline, then you need to get started very early, at least a year ahead of time.

4. Researchers should use the utmost respect when trying to acquire informants. You may never find someone who wants to talk with you. Why would a Native wish to reveal information to a researcher who comes across as arrogant because he/she is university educated? Why talk to someone who acts like he/she already knows everything about the tribe? Why talk to someone who shows no respect for the informant's family? The answers to these questions are obvious. But what if you are respectful and genuinely want to learn? How can you convince the informant that you mean well? Ultimately, keep in mind this question: Why should a Native tell you anything at all?

5. Use caution when using cameras and tape recorders. Make certain that informants understand what you will do with the pictures or tapes. Natives are like everyone else (except those who participate on reality television shows) in that they don't want strangers taking their pictures for the benefit of those strangers. Always ask permission and be prepared to pay. If you arrive on a reservation or other tribal land with a camera or tape recorder, it may be taken away from you. If you plan on interviewing someone (and he/she has agreed) then find out ahead of time if he/she minds being recorded.

6. Informants should be given fair and appropriate return. Why would anyone give you information if he/she isn't going to receive anything in return for helping you? For decades anthropologists and other writers have treated Natives as second-class citizens and as objects of research that should be thrilled to be the focus of a book or essay. If you plan to ask for an interview, a photograph, or a family history, be prepared to pay for it either in the form of money, copies of the book, or an acknowledgment. You can make an offer, but it is up to your informer to name the price. And no, a bead necklace is not adequate payment.

7. Every attempt should be made to cooperate with the current host society. It is extremely frustrating for writers to go through the tribal research guidelines committee, adhere to protocol, and be prepared to give payment for information, only to encounter a big roadblock just as they prepare to write or even turn in their last draft to their publisher. Like the U.S. government, most tribal governments have elections to determine their leaders. A writer might make an agreement with one political faction, only to watch that faction fall out of favor with voters and another arrive that does not approve of the research. Some people forge ahead and proceed with their research knowing they are taking a chance. My advice is to steer clear of unstable tribes. Otherwise, you're in for a great deal of frustration.

8. Physical anthropologists, archaeologists, and other researchers wishing to desecrate Indian burials in order to study Indian remains and funerary objects should obtain permission to do so from tribes. Another hotly contested issue in Native Studies is the removal of sacred cultural items and skeletal remains for "study." Many anthropologists maintain that this "study" benefits humankind, whereas Natives argue – rightfully so – that there has never been anything discovered in a tribal burial that has helped anyone except those who need the job of studying them. Natives view this practice as nothing less than grave robbing. If your writing depends on gathering data from burials, then either change your topic or secure permission from tribal authorities before proceeding.

9. Results of the study should be reviewed by the tribe's elected representatives and religious leaders. This is a step that almost all researchers ignore because they refuse to allow nonscholars and non-writers to approve/disapprove their work. Many researchers believe that their university degree gives them license to publish anything and everything they want. But consider how Natives feel when they give a

77

researcher information, only to find it twisted into a text that is incorrect. Writers of memoirs and biographies need the Native individuals in question (or a representative) to approve the text and vouch for the accuracy of details; writers of histories and ethnographies need to permit the appropriate tribal organization or authority figure to inspect and approve their work before publication.

10. **The researcher must follow the guidelines for each new project.** Even if you had a successful experience with your first project, that does not mean the tribe will allow you to do a second project. And just because one tribe welcomed you does not mean the tribe down the freeway will, too. You must start all over again for each project.

Other Guidelines to Keep in Mind

Other principles beyond the above guidelines need to gird your research and writing if it is to be sensitive and successful.

PLAGIARISM

Plagiarism is stealing. Make certain you do not use a quote or a passage from another work without properly citing that work. I could list several dozen examples from my and colleagues' classes in which students lifted quotes from books and essays without giving credit to who actually wrote them. I also can cite a few passages from books about Natives that were lifted – without citing – from my published works. Plagiarism is a form of cheating and if you get caught, you can flunk your class, be excused from school, lose a book contract, and even lose your job. Don't do it.

GIVING CREDIT WHERE IT IS DUE

Very close to plagiarism is using ideologies and discussion topics you have read in another work and then writing about those ideas to give the impression that you are the one who came up with them. Several books about Natives have been published recently that do just this; the authors neglect to cite previous writings about research guidelines, literary criticism, American Indian studies programs, activism, decolonization, and sovereignty. While this is not literally plagiarism, it is unprofessional behavior and guilty parties will eventually find their unethical methodologies discussed in critical book reviews.

CLAIMING INDIANNESS

Library shelves have many books written by individuals who claim to be Native but aren't. If you are not tribally enrolled and without strong tribal connections but say you are in order to sell more copies of your book, then advertising yourself as an Indian author is fraudulent and unethical.

Unless you are Native, you do not know what it is like to be a Native and you have not encountered the same racism, prejudice, and discrimination that Natives have. You can, however, write sympathetically about Indians. You can write from a non-Native perspective about the problems you have witnessed and propose solutions. But do not try to put yourself into shoes that don't fit. Natives (and knowledgeable allies) will pick up on your scheme in a second. Ethnic fraud is a serious problem in the area of Native Studies, but it has also expanded into the world of nonacademic publishing. If you try and market yourself as something you are not, Natives will know and will attempt to expose you. Better to be honest.

USING AN "INDIAN FRIEND"

Many authors try to enhance their work by saying they had a Native informer or friend who educated them about the ways of tribal America. It is one thing to have Native informers who talk about their history and culture because they have an agreement with the author. It is quite another to fabricate or misuse a Native to make a profit. Some authors have hit the jackpot by claiming that a traditional, "wise" Native who inexplicably lives far from his/her homeland decided to bestow the author with all kinds of secretive wisdom instead of confiding in a member of his/her tribe. Only readers ignorant of Natives fall for this. Unfortunately, many have money in their pockets.

DO NOT TRY TO DECEIVE READERS

Do not thank Indians in your acknowledgment page unless they actually contributed to your work. I have been thanked in several books this past year, but I'm not sure why. If this is a strategy you have in mind to keep those "thanked people" from giving you a critical book review, think again. This plan is transparent and may anger the people you are trying to placate. On the same note, do not purport in your introduction to include certain items in your book (such as "using Native voice") when those things are not in there at all.

Q & A

Q: *How is it that many researchers get past the requirement of submitting their project proposal to their school's* IRB *or the tribe's Research Board* (RB)?

A: Easy. There is no law that says you have to. Many unscrupulous writers and scholars do not think they need anyone to dictate what they can and cannot write about, which is why these guidelines were created in the first place. Be sure you're not in this category of writers.

CHAPTER SEVEN

Editing Your Work

Everyone, no matter how skilled in writing, must edit his/her work. Rarely can a writer create an adequate product in only one draft. I'm not the only writer who has become frustrated by editing my writing – sometimes rewriting a dozen times – only to find yet another error after the "final" read. I estimate that research is 20 percent of my work. The first draft is never particularly daunting to write and takes up 10 percent of the energy, while editing and rewriting is 70 percent of my effort. Some writers feel that they can rewrite endlessly, but you have to cut it off someplace and hope you have done the best you can.

A colleague of mine who wrote a book on Indians in Kansas expressed his dismay to me that the finished book stated the Civil War started in 1961. Whose fault is this? A finger could be pointed at the author and the copyeditor and/or proofreader and even the editor. Another friend who wrote more than twenty nonacademic books (including fiction, romance, and military history) before his death told me that all the author has to do is submit a book with great content and the copyeditor takes care of the rest. I disagree. No one is perfect, not even a skilled copyeditor. You should not leave it up to others to correct your mistakes, not even those whom you pay to edit your work. Some presses are garnering reputations at being careless at proofing and you don't want to contribute to that image. You do the best you can before you submit the manuscript. This saves time, energy, and aggravation for the person hired to edit your work.

Content and Presentation

For both journal and book submissions it is crucial that authors send their best work, not a messy draft that promises something wonderful in the future. Editors have no time for promises.

● Double-check your sources. Many scholars make the mistake of citing a secondary source, that is, they take a "fact" from another book then cite that book. You must always look at the sources that author used and then scrutinize them. It is surprising how many errors authors make, and it is your responsibility to make certain that you don't copy them. Some books have become models of copying: that is, the authors merely cite each other.

● Be sure the footnotes match the text.

● Make sure your title adequately conveys what is in the book and that it does not promise more than you can deliver.

● Double-space and print only on one side of clean paper.

● Be sure the pages are right-side up, accounted for, in order, and numbered.

● Check and recheck for grammar and spelling errors.

● Read the work out loud or have someone read it to you. For both fiction and nonfiction, you can catch many errors hearing the work read out loud.

● Do not include everything you found about a topic and do not belabor any issue. Knowing what to exclude is as important as knowing what to include.

● Omit words if doing so does not alter the meaning of the text. If you can lose an entire sentence, do the same thing, no matter how much you like that sentence. You can always use it in another work. Don't fret about losing that great statement forever. Louise Erdrich has said that she refers to discarded work, that is, "old wrecks," like a car junkyard where she finds parts for a new work.

● Be creative in your descriptors. You don't want to overuse adjectives or adverbs, so try and pick words that colorfully describe the action.

● Don't use passive voice when you can use active voice. Instead of "the dog was covered with fleas," consider "fleas covered the dog."

● Try to omit "it was," "there are," and similar constructions. Instead of "The day was hot and dry," perhaps use "the hot, dry day."

● Avoid repeating words. Use your thesaurus and be creative with synonyms.

● Keep long quotes to a minimum. While short phrases can add punch to your work, block quotes should be used only when the quote is unique and essential to your point.

● Look at your draft from the perspective of a reader. You may think you have covered your bases and have said everything you need to. But have you completely told your story?

● Make sure your dialogue sounds realistic. Do people really say "do not" and "cannot"?

● Check your dates, facts, and figures. If you are using percentages, make certain they add up properly.

● Edit your work from a hard copy. Even if your computer contains spell/word/grammar check, you must double-check for errors. Sometimes your computer does not know whether you meant to use "and" or "had." Plus, you must check for content.

● Make sure your sentences are not too long. A paragraph is usually composed of two to four sentences. Don't make the mistake of having one long, sixty-word sentence. That's hard to read. Similarly, long paragraphs are difficult to read and often drag out explanations more than is necessary.

● Check to see in your fiction work if you have included too many characters. Unless each one has a significant role to play, drop them.

● Don't use fancy writing or verbal gymnastics. Many people, academics included, are not interested in reading many scholarly works because the language used is incomprehensible. It is one thing to use technical jargon where it is needed but another when the author aggressively uses the thesaurus in order to appear more intelligent than the readers. It is impressive enough (and difficult enough) to use straightforward language in explaining complicated events or situations with basic words in unique ways than to use archaic, cumbersome lingo. Use short words instead of long ones.

● Make sure you thoroughly explain yourself. Academics must define terms. There are several ways to do this: you can supply a glossary; explain a term in a note; or, best of all, explain the meaning in the text.

● Don't refer to a group of people in the singular. If you refer to the Cherokee tribe, for example, you can write "Cherokee tribe," but if you are referring to group of Cherokees, write "Cherokees," not "Cherokee." Animals are often referred to in the singular when one actually means more than one. Don't make the mistake of lumping Natives into the same group the same way we do with animals.

● Find your own style. There is, for example, only one Gerald Vizenor.

You may admire his work, but you probably cannot imitate his unique writing style.

- Use statistics when you can. They strengthen your arguments.
- Have more than one set of eyes read through your manuscript. Enlist the aid of your colleagues, major professor, or writing group to edit your paper. I learned a strange but effective editing technique in graduate school. Many competitive students love to make their fellow students look bad. This is compounded by the terrific stress and fear that most graduate students feel when job-hunting time draws near. I realized that the best people to edit my work were those who wanted to make certain that I knew I had made mistakes. Enlist someone you know who has a beef with you and you just may receive the best, most thorough thesis, dissertation, article, and/or grant proposal editing of your career!

Identify Yourself and Your Sources

My students are taught that when they are composing a review of a book, one of the first things they must investigate is the author. Although traditional scholars will argue that nonfiction work, if properly created, will be unbiased and objective, no writer of Native history and culture is truly unbiased.

You should, in your introduction, firmly identify yourself. If you are Native, then you should state that you are tribally enrolled and describe your allegiance to your tribe. If you are non-Native, then say so and describe why you felt compelled to write your project. Many people write about Natives because they "have always been interested in Indians," but that does not mean they know much about them. Admit that you are learning and that your work is not the definitive piece. This is helpful and honest.

If I pick up a book about Hopis and read that the author did not talk with Hopis, did not secure permission to do research from the tribe, and only looked in the library for information, I have no interest in reading that book. Many scholars and writers balk at having to identify their stance mainly because it can cost them book royalties, but it is important information for readers.

More Reasons to Identify Yourself

● There are too many examples of biased, unbalanced work to prove the point that most writers of Native history cannot write with the best interests of Natives in mind. Fortunately, there are many writers who write to correct misinformation, to assist tribes by finding traditional knowledge to help solve modern-day problems, to locate information that might help with land claims, and so on. They write with an agenda in mind, just as the anti-Indian writers do. Subjectivity is a reality of writing these days, so you may as well tell us about yourself at the onset.

● Readers no longer believe authors are purely objective in gathering data, interpreting the data, and composing stories about tribal peoples. Readers are looking for books written from the "Indian perspective," "tribal perspective," or "outsider's perspective." Many traditional scholars cringe at the thought that they must tell readers why they are working on a particular project, but in actuality, there is nothing wrong – and everything helpful – in positioning yourself as an author.

● Volatile arguments exist between Natives and non-Native scholars about authoritative voice – that is, who actually "knows" about the topic – and the two camps want to know precisely where that author stands.

● Readers, especially Native readers, desire to know who is doing the writing because they are aware that most Native writers (and many non-Native writers) will be more inclusive in their writings. They know that some writers will include tribal perspectives, and that is what they prefer to read about.

● Informed readers will want to look at books about a topic from several viewpoints.

Q & A

Q: *Can I contact a prominent writer and ask him/her to read my work and give comments?*

A: You can try, but do not expect him/her to say yes. There are copy-editors who do this kind of work for a living. Some charge by the word, some by the page or manuscript. University presses pay readers to review submissions. Why would a person do this time-consuming work for free for someone he/she does not even know?

While many established writers do want to help junior writers, keep in mind that these writers are established because they write a lot. That means they're busy. Your invitation also puts them in the tough position of saying "no." I say "tough position" because they know that their refusal makes them appear unhelpful.

During the year prior to my writing this book, I was asked to read two master's theses, a dissertation draft, and an entire book draft; to answer two sets of questions about Native America (each set was at least twenty questions long); and to participate in two interviews for dissertation research. In the two days that I edited the last chapter of this book, my e-mail ding-donged and I received four more requests from graduate students not from my university to critique their theses and dissertations. All of these requests were made by students I do not know, and I was not offered any compensation. I know from experience that if a busy writer acquiesces and does this kind of work (and, indeed, it is work), you may not get thanked in any introduction and your ideas might get lifted without your receiving any credit or citation.

Some students become indignant when they are turned away. Some believe that because a scholar is a full professor and has a long list of publications that somehow that scholar no longer feels pressure to write and now can devote his/her time to reading the works of younger scholars and encouraging them. This is absolutely not the case. Most of us are overwhelmed with writing and speaking commitments. As much as we appreciate that you like our work, and indeed, as much as we want to see junior scholars succeed, we simply cannot tend to every person who wants our attention.

CHAPTER EIGHT

Submitting Your Work to Journals

Now that you have completed your essay about Indigenous history, culture, or current events (book manuscripts are discussed in the next chapter), where will you send it? How will you send it? Are you aware of the various journals' guidelines?

Meet the Needs of the Journal

Look at the journal's Web page, or request guidelines to ensure that you won't waste your and the journal editor's time. I get five or six essays per month that have nothing to do with what *AIQ* publishes. For example, I have received papers dealing with India, German history, and Viagra. For two years I did not accept essays dealing with specific fiction authors and topics; this information was posted clearly on the *AIQ* Web page. Yet I still received dozens of papers on those very topics. Receiving unwanted papers means that the editor or assistant editor must spend time writing to authors to remind them of the guidelines. Larger journals often throw away unwanted submissions without contacting the author.

Before sending your paper off to a journal and even as you are writing your piece, you need to keep in mind what the editor and reviewers of your paper will look for. Below are the most pertinent instructions for reviewers for *AIQ*. Although other academic journals have their own comment guidelines, they read pretty much like ours.

Read the questions our reviewers answer and ask yourself if your article measures up to these criteria. As an author, you should go through this list and make certain that the answers are positive to the best of your ability.

Instructions for Reviewers of *American Indian Quarterly*

EVALUATION CRITERIA

In responding to these more specific criteria, please keep in mind that *AIQ* is an interdisciplinary journal. This means that for any given article, most of our readers will not be specialists in that particular topic area or discipline. We are especially interested in articles that demonstrate a depth of scholarship in a specific topic and discipline but that also have a broader appeal to readers outside those specialties. We also want to encourage alternative approaches to American Indian Studies that do not conform to established disciplinary practices but nevertheless demonstrate sound scholarship.

1. Scholarship
— shows originality of thought
— makes appropriate use of relevant literature
— provides adequate documentation and acknowledgment of sources
— presents sufficient interpretive foreground and contextual background
— uses an appropriate methodology that is clearly described
— is likely to be cited in subsequent works on the same topic

2. Relevance
— expands or enriches the knowledge or ideas about that focus is likely to be read by a broad segment of the journal's readership falls within the general area of American Indian or Native American Studies explores a focus that is of central rather than peripheral significance within the general area

3. Style
— is well written
— is clearly and logically organized
— contains appropriate examples
— uses a minimum of jargon
— is likely to be understood on a first reading by journal readers who are not specialists in the area

4. Impressions
— Did this article change the way in which you thought about the topic?
— Did this article make you want to read other works by the same author?
— Would you read this article through to its conclusion if you discovered it in a journal?

Read your completed essay again with a critical eye, putting yourself in the readers' shoes and answer the above questions honestly. If you do not know how to answer the questions because you aren't familiar with the field, then you need to scrap the piece and start over after you spend much time reading and researching.

Follow the Rules

Regardless of the size of the publishing house or journal, some "rules and regulations" are consistent. A good way to learn submission protocol is to look at recent editions of the instructional Writer's Guide books published by Writer's Digest Books (http://www.writersmarket.com). These books contain lists of book and journal publishers along with specific information about submission format, what topics publishers are interested in, and their contract terms. Many of these publishing houses and journals receive thousands of submissions a year and strict submission guidelines are crucial in order for them to manage the mounds of paper that pile up on the editors' and their assistants' desks.

Publishers mean exactly what they write. For example, if their guidelines say, "We do not answer queries or manuscripts which do not have an SASE (self-addressed stamped envelope) attached," that means if you do not enclose an envelope that is stamped and addressed to you (so that they can send you a reply at your expense), then you'll never hear from that publisher. The reason for this is monetary. Presses simply don't have the money to foot the bill for every aspect of the publication process. The least the author can do is supply an SASE.

Some journals, like AIQ, and smaller presses, such as some university presses, are not as strict in their guidelines. But they do have some rules and they are meant to be followed. If you don't adhere to the rules, then it may be assumed by the editorial staff that you are careless, rude, and may not write well.

Presentation Counts

Pay close attention to presentation because great writing is not enough. Every manuscript should adhere to the following:

- Keep the papers unfolded and free of coffee stains.
- Type on one side of white paper.
- Double-space your work, even footnotes, endnotes, and block quotes.
- Use an easy – to-read type such as Times. Do not use cursive and do not use all capitals. Both styles are difficult to read. If editors cannot easily read your paper, then they will not even try.
- Use 12-point type. Any smaller is hard to read and any larger looks like you're trying to stretch the work.
- Number your pages in the top right corner.
- Unless otherwise specified by the publisher's guidelines, put your name only on the cover page.
- Either staple or paper clip your pages together. Some journals specify "no staples," and I know of no journal that wants to receive a submission in a three-ring notebook or other form of binder. A simple brown envelope that is not taped or stapled shut is the best package.
- Never enclose original drawings or photographs until your paper is accepted and the editor is expecting you to send them. Send copies with your proposal.
- Include a cover letter to briefly introduce yourself. If you are a published writer you can enclose a brief history of your writings, but a lengthy résumé is not necessary. Briefly discuss your topic (fiction, nonfiction) and include a paragraph that succinctly summarizes the work. Insert a sentence that tells the editor the page length and word count. Make certain that you include the date, as well as your title, address, phone number, and e-mail address. Sign your letter.
- The current manuscript is what editors want to look at, so do not enclose copies of past publications, book cover ideas, marketing strategies, food, or gifts.

● See chapter 7 for suggestions about how to ensure your work is as polished as possible.

● If the journal guidelines say that the journal will only consider looking at a paper that is no more than 35 double-spaced pages, don't send a 50-page, single-spaced paper. Also, don't try and slip the notes past in a separate format. I often get a 35-page paper that is indeed 35 pages of text, but the notes are another 10 pages printed in a tiny type size and are single spaced. That makes the essay way too long. Most journals have tight restrictions because they can only include a certain number of papers in each issue.

● Journals will specify the style in which the submission should be written. Most like the *Chicago Manual of Style*, 15th edition. If that's what they say in the guidelines, then don't present the editor with something else just because you like it better.

● If the guidelines say send four copies, then send four copies. Most publishing houses and, certainly, journal offices are now in a budget crunch. If I receive one copy of a submission that means I have to make three more copies and charge the costs to my college, which makes the dean unhappy. Plus, it makes for more competition for the college office copy machine. Even major publishers need to save money, and chances are they will not consider your paper if you do not send as many copies as they ask for. Some journals allow e-mail submissions, but check before you send one.

Other Journal Submission Protocol

DO NOT CONTACT THE EDITOR

Do not contact the editor of your selected journal and ask if he/she would like to publish your essay. Do not contact the editor and ask if he/she will critique your essay before you submit it. Editors can tell you if they like your paper idea, but they cannot tell you if they will publish it. Most academic journals such as AIQ are refereed, that is, papers are sent out to reviewers who specialize in the topic for critical evaluation. This is one of the most difficult aspects of editing a journal. I receive these kinds of queries from people I know each month, and it puts me in a difficult situation. Editors may like your paper and they may like you, but they cannot make a unilateral decision without carefully considering the reviewer commentaries. Editors also do not have time to offer suggestions unless you formally submit your paper. Many editors know that if they do critique your paper, then you may send it elsewhere and much time will have been wasted.

FOLLOW COMMUNICATION INSTRUCTIONS

If you are interested in finding out if your paper is acceptable as a submission and you want to call the editor to talk about it, listen carefully to the phone message at the journal office. The message on my office voicemail recording clearly says, "Do not leave messages regarding *AIQ* on this line." I give the journal office number, yet many authors leave a message on my line anyway. Same with e-mails. I cannot handle my work (as a professor and writer) and *AIQ* work on one e-mail address. Often, I will erase e-mail and phone messages if the author has not followed my clear instructions. Larger publishers will not even answer your call or will ignore it. Be sure to honor publishers and editors' requests regarding communications.

BE PATIENT

Rest assured that journal editors and book publishers want good material and they are hopeful they can accept your submission. At *AIQ*, we work as fast as we can to get submissions. Calling repeatedly won't make the process go faster, and repeated calls are annoying. As soon as you send off your work, immediately start on the next project. If you wait months until you receive good news about one submission before starting another, you won't get many writing projects completed.

An exception to calling the editor is when your submission has been at the journal past the time the editor has told you to expect an answer. As a rule of thumb, when you send off your submission note on your calendar the date you mailed it. Then flip ahead on your calendar one month beyond the time the editor told you to expect a reply and note on the calendar that it's time contact him/her. Most editors try hard to get on-time reviews, but we are at the mercy of the reviewers. At *AIQ*, we often have to contact late reviewers five or six times, often to no avail.

BE CAREFUL WITH SIMULTANEOUS SUBMISSIONS

Because the review process can take months, some authors wonder if they should send their paper to several places at once. After all, if an author is rejected by the first publisher after three months, then that author might have to wait another three months for an answer from the next publisher. The problem with simultaneous submissions, however, is that refereed journals send the submissions out for review to scholars who are not paid for their services. It takes time to carefully read a manuscript and it is not good news for an editor to hear from the author that the author plans to take his/her essay elsewhere because another journal gave an answer faster. The author should always ask if simultaneous submissions are allowed.

BE CAREFUL WITH TERM PAPERS

Graduate students should not submit a term paper, class paper, or chapter from a thesis or dissertation unless it is truly exceptional in both content and writing style, and it can "stand alone" as a distinct, informative essay from start to finish. Graduate students should rework their papers and have their mentors review them before sending them off. An A on a class paper may ensure an A in the class, but that high class grade does not mean it's worthy of publication.

INCLUDE A COVER LETTER

Include a cover letter that states your name and contact information, including your e-mail address and where you will be a few months from the time of your submission. After receiving the requisite four copies, we do most of our business through e-mail (to save time and money). Probably 10 percent of the papers I receive as *AIQ* submissions have no contact information enclosed and we have to locate the author's name and address on the envelope. Not providing an e-mail address slows down the process considerably. Not sending a cover letter with contact information is unprofessional and leaves a bad impression. Editors might think that if you have no time to write a formal, professional letter, you don't have time to be professional in the way you write your paper. Mentors take note: graduate students and new professors, especially, are guilty of this.

POLITENESS COUNTS

Spell the name of the editor correctly. While I realize that Mihesuah is not the easiest name to remember, there is no reason to be disrespectful. I get many letters addressing me as "Mr." I'm not male and I am "Professor" or "Dr." Spelling my name incorrectly automatically makes me think that the person is not careful in his/her research. I don't reject papers because someone has referred to me as "Mr. Myeswaza," but if it comes down to a split decision based on the reviewers' comments, I will decide no. Other editors with equally complex names have less patience with such disrespect and will deposit the manuscript in the nearest trash receptacle without further consideration.

DON'T TRY TO USE YOUR BIG NAME TO GET PUBLISHED

Having numerous publications under your belt does not mean that everything you churn out is publishable. Several years ago I received an essay submission from a well-published author. The paper was half handwritten, half typed (with countless typos), with handwriting in all four margins and on yellow self-adhesive notes. There was no cover letter, only a note written in red marker on orange construction paper (half a torn sheet). After informing the author that I liked her idea but that her paper must be submitted properly, I never heard from her again.

Another set of coeditors sent me a set of essays for a special issue on a specified theme in Native Studies. With the exception of a few of the papers, the collection was poorly written, unoriginal, and mind-numbing, especially a twelve-page, double-columned poem. Worse, the editors said they had indeed sent the papers out for review – to each other. After rejecting said special issue, I was berated. The "editors" told me that I should not have rejected their effort because "they were the experts on this topic." Obviously, if that really were the case, the submission would have been much different.

A more recent incident involves an oft-published Native fiction writer who took exception to the AIQ author permission form. She misunderstood the passage that clearly states an AIQ author will always be able to publish his/her essay elsewhere, and without bothering to ask for clarification she proceeded to demand that her essay be pulled. It is doubtful that anyone else who knows about this incident (her

94

unprofessional language included) will be eager to take her on as one of their authors.

Writers who have a solid publishing history should never abandon courtesy, protocol, and good work. Like the author who submitted a (rejected) paper last year on a tired topic and called me repeatedly to ask me if I had accepted it or not and expected me to because, as he/she put it, "I'm a well-known author and everyone reads my work," your name may get you in the door but your work and attitude are what allow you to stay in the room.

DON'T TRY TO WIN THE EXCESSIVE PACKAGING AWARD

Last year the *AIQ* office received a box only a bit smaller than those that hold reams of copy paper. After struggling to cut open the layers of packing tape, I discovered another bubble-wrapped parcel. Thinking this might be glass or ceramic, I again gritted my teeth to carefully cut away the layer upon layer of packing to tape to find nothing more than a twenty-page paper – and a badly written one at that.

No matter how important and delicate you think your words are, please don't send any editor a heavily wrapped package that takes more than a few seconds to open. This means

● Do not use enough packing tape to waterproof your manila envelope (or small box that contains your submission).

● Do not use white squishy packing material pieces.

● Do not use envelopes with stuffing that sheds all over.

● Do not tape all four sides of an envelope; this is excessive, unnecessary, and annoying.

● Do use an envelope only large enough for your submission and seal it with only one strip of Scotch tape. If you're concerned that your paper might become bent in transit, insert one piece of cardboard into the envelope.

USE OVERNIGHT DELIVERY SPARINGLY

Fancy packaging and overnight delivery may indeed get the editors' attention, although not in the way you want. *AIQ* receives numerous FedEx envelopes per year; however, most contain only submissions. Unless the editor has already accepted your paper and you are sending him/her your final version that must be sent to the copyeditor in a few days, there is no reason to send anything faster than first-class mail. It is understandable that many writers are thrilled to complete a project and they want an editor to look at it immediately, but the truth is that editor probably will put your envelope on his/her desk where it will sit with the other submissions until someone can read it.

Q & A

Q: *Why is the editor taking so long to respond to my submission?*

A: It may appear to writers that journal editors take forever to make their decisions and are doing nothing, but I assure you that they are constantly reading submissions, making comments on them, and thinking about how to fill issues with quality essays and about whom to solicit for papers, commentaries, and potential special issues. They are very busy and aren't purposely ignoring you.

CHAPTER NINE

Submitting Your Work to a Book Publisher

Submitting your manuscript about American Indians to a book publisher is much the same as submitting an essay to a journal, but there are important differences. Keep in mind that no matter what kind of work writers produce, they generally go through the same process.

Sending your very best work is a must, but whereas journal editors want to see a finished product, sometimes (especially if you are an author with an established track record) book publishers will award an author an advance contract based on a well-developed idea for a book. That idea is presented in a proposal, which can be subject to the same review process as a normal book-length manuscript. An advance contract is attractive since it gets a publisher to commit to your work early on during the planning and research stage and it certainly strengthens one's curriculum vitae (cv) or résumé. Do keep in mind, however, that your eventually completed manuscript will still be subject to review and that an advance contract will not guarantee publication if the finished manuscript is found lacking by press staff or reviewers.

The review and contract processes in book publishing are more complex and lengthy than they are in journal publishing. For example, after reviews of a manuscript have been completed and received at a university press (for an explanation of what that is, see below), the editorial staff usually meets to discuss, evaluate, and endorse or reject each other's book projects. Sometimes the press director and staff from other departments such as marketing are present and have a vote. At this internal press meeting, some book manuscripts likely will be rejected. Furthermore, most university presses are governed by an advisory board, which has the final say as to whether a manuscript will be published. A press's advisory board is usually made up of faculty and administrators from the press's host university. Editors of a press meet regularly (the frequency of meeting varies from every month to four times a year) with the advisory board, who read and consider the reviews of book manuscripts, the author's CV, and the author's written response to suggestions made in the reviews. The advisory board then votes on whether to offer a contract for the project. So, remember, even if your acquisition editor supports your work, the ultimate fate of your manuscript at a university press is in the hands of the press's boss, the advisory board.

How to Determine Who Might Publish Your Work

There are four general types of presses that potentially would be interested in publishing your work on American Indians:

   ~ 1. *University presses* are nonprofit presses, each of which is affiliated with a host university (or consortium of universities), such as the University of Pennsylvania or University of Nebraska–Lincoln. Some university presses have built strong, in-depth, and nationally recognized lists of publications on and about American Indians. Their original and still primary goal is to publish scholarship, collections of historical documents, and, for some, textbooks for college classes. But the types of books they publish are changing. Given an industry-wide decline in library sales and reduced university and state funding in recent years, university presses are increasingly seeking alternate forms of publication to subsidize their missions. Consequently, most university presses today, while still academic, are also open to books that appeal to a broader audience than only scholars.

Why publish with a university press? If your work is academic, then such presses will best recognize the value of your work and understand your audience. The smaller size of a university press often means that the staff will be available for substantive discussions and forthcoming with suggestions; you and your work will receive a respectable level of attention, from editing through design. Because most university presses are less concerned with high profit ratios than are commercial presses, university presses can potentially take greater chances on noteworthy books with less-than-promising sales prospects, and it is also likely that your book will remain in print longer than if issued by a commercial house. The chief disadvantages of this type of press should be apparent – they cannot afford large advances or sizable royalties, their print runs are usually modest at best, and their marketing efforts are necessarily on a smaller scale than those of a commercial press. Also be aware that the academic background of university presses means that some will not be receptive to book projects that are considered "nonscholarly," such as works of fiction or those lacking footnotes. Certainly not all university presses are this rigid, and research and inquiries should help you identify those most interested in your type of book.

~ 2. *Commercial presses* are for-profit companies that usually publish a wide range of books and related products designed to earn revenue. Commercial presses such as Random House or Simon and Schuster can be enormous, maintaining a number of subdivisions called imprints, each with its own specialty; frequently the press itself is part of an even greater, international conglomerate. Books by and about American Indians do appear from commercial presses but in far smaller numbers than from university presses.

Why publish with a commercial press? If you have written that rare manuscript that you believe has strong potential to attract a large readership and make money, then a commercial press could serve your interests well. They can afford sizable advances and more generous royalty terms than can university presses, and their marketing clout can be staggering. Commercial presses can also afford to pay for book-signing tours and author interviews.

The tradeoff is often the level of attention and quality of treatment given your book. Your book is only one of a huge number of books these presses publish each year. If yearly sales decline below a certain threshold, there is little incentive for a commercial press to keep your book in print. Please also keep in mind that many of these presses do not have a great deal of experience editing, designing, or marketing American Indian books, so misunderstandings and unhappy compromises may occur as your manuscript becomes a book.

In considering fiction and nonfiction books about Natives, some commercial presses insist on the inclusion of stereotypical characters, plots, and images in order to attract a mainstream audience. You must consider carefully whether you are willing to sacrifice integrity for money.

ოთ 3. *Local presses* nicely serve authors whose book topics are regional in focus – such as a locally textured biography of an aged county resident – instead of relevant more broadly to the national or international readership reached by university and commercial presses. Local presses are small, with very tight budgets and usually little money for editing, production, and promotion. Such presses are usually not considered as prestigious as university and commercial presses by academic employers.

Why publish with a local press? Associated sometimes with independent bookstores, they frequently boast an effective network of contacts within their city or region; they usually know their local audience very well. Rather than using these presses as a backup when all else fails, be realistic about the scope of your work and its audience – perhaps a local press is best for your book.

ოთ 4. *Vanity presses* (sometimes known as self-publishing presses, although some writers find and pay their own printer and are literally "self-published") publish your book, but you pay all of the costs of publication, advertisement, and distribution. The self-publishing industry has grown considerably in recent years. Why publish with a vanity press? Many wonderful books are self-published, and some talented authors with money to spend self-publish in order to control better their book's editing, design, and royalties. Some tribal organizations prefer to retain such control and, rather than work with a university or commercial press, will arrange the publication of their own histories and narratives themselves.

But be aware of the limitations in going it alone in this way. Vanity companies make their profit more from the authors who pay them up front than from readers buying books. Look carefully at costs, what vanity presses do and don't do, and what you are responsible for. Some vanity presses produce books in an electronic form only, some publish regular print books, and some "on-demand" publishers do both, storing your book electronically and not printing a copy until it is actually ordered. Self-publishing is often very expensive, with no guarantee that you will break even – let alone profit – from your work. And it is all on your shoulders – you and not the press are responsible for the final version, so you'd better check thoroughly for typos and grammatical errors. Self-published books often lack developed design expertise and thus can look rough and homespun to bookstores and potential readers. Also keep in mind that many bookstores do not stock self-published books, preferring to do business with known publishing houses and established contacts. One last word of caution – there is a stigma associated with self-publishing. Academic employers and established publishers most of the time don't consider a vanity publication to be viable and will ask, Why can't you get a publisher to take your work? Is it not good enough? Sadly, these questions are valid – many self-published works are truly awful.

Which Book Publisher Is the Right One?

Before you bundle up that manuscript and mail it off, make certain that the press to whom you are sending your work is appropriate for you and your work. Your first major step in publishing is to preselect a handful of presses most likely to be interested in your book manuscript. It may take a while to figure out the best press for you, but the time will be well spent. If you are now shopping for a press, here are four tips to narrow your choices.

TIP 1: Find a press that already publishes books on your subject. This sounds obvious, but a common complaint among publishers is that they receive streams of submissions everyday that have absolutely nothing to do with their list interests. Publishers such as university presses don't rush to print every interesting book manuscript they receive. Rather than taking a scattershot approach, they specialize in certain types of books and are interested only in particular fields of scholarship and selected topics. Manuscripts and proposals that fall outside those areas of interest are usually rejected immediately. Your chances of getting published will increase dramatically if you learn a press's list – its areas of specialization and interest. Think about it – it would be a waste of time to send a fiction submission to a press if it doesn't publish fiction or submit a manuscript about revisionist perspectives on Custer if a press doesn't consider historical or current multicultural topics. Also understand that you will be better served by a press specializing in your area because of its developed editorial, design, and marketing experience. The press's marketing department will already know the appropriate journals in which to advertise your book and to whom to send review copies; and a recognized publishing reputation will encourage sales of new books. Take time to become acquainted with the lists of a range of presses and then match your manuscript to the most appropriate list or lists.

How do you find out the areas of specialization and interests of publishers, especially those who would most likely be interested in your work? Try these three sources of information:

∾ 1. *Bookshelves and bibliographies.* Note the publishers of the books on your bookshelves, especially books you consulted or referenced when researching and writing. For example, if you have written a manuscript on Native water rights, which presses published earlier or contemporary books on the topic? Chances are that the publishers interested in those books will want to hear from you. Also look at the bibliographies in those books; there may be additional relevant books on the same topic listed there. Do keep in mind that you want to focus on a press's new book titles, known as its frontlist, rather than its older books in print, known as its backlist. Books published within the last three years will more likely reflect a press's current areas of specialization and interest than older titles.

∾ 2. *Publisher Web pages.* Go on-line and become even more informed before submitting your manuscript. A great place to learn about the types of books and topics favored by a press is its Web page on the Internet. Most publisher Web pages feature current seasonal catalogs, new books and active series, and a list of contacts. A helpful organization for learning more about university presses is the Association of American University Presses, which maintains a list of current university presses and links to their Web pages at the site http://aaupnet.org/membership/directory.html. Listings like the *Writers Market* give indispensable information about publishers, especially commercial presses.

∾ 3. *Conferences.* A good way to learn the specialties of publishers is to attend academic conferences that are related to the subject of your book manuscript. Conferences related to American Indians include the American Society for Ethnohistory, Organization of American Historians, Western History Association, and the American Anthropological Association. Fiction writers can submit their work to university presses, but as stated previously, many such presses are highly selective. Many other publishers of fiction have booths at writers' conferences, as well as meeting times when writers can briefly discuss their proposals with potential editors. Publishers regularly exhibit their current books at such conferences, so make it a priority to track down the exhibit hall or room containing their displays. A publisher's exhibit of books at a conference features recent catalogs and neatly showcases what they are currently doing and which books and series they regard as most significant.

TIP 2: Find an acquiring editor you can work with and trust. Acquisition editors discover and sign quality, publishable manuscripts for their press. They identify projects by traveling to conferences, reading selected journals and magazines, browsing dissertation abstracts, reading unsolicited letters and e-mails, listening to and following up on advice and tips from scholars and authors, and even commissioning books themselves. Some editors are scholars and authors in their own right, often having advance degrees in one of their areas of acquisitions; others have concentrated their professional careers solely on publishing. All are very busy, all of the time.

From the beginning of contact with a press through the review, acceptance (we hope), and submission of a final manuscript, your main contact will be an acquisition editor (and sometimes his/her assistant). Since you must work closely with that editor for months and often years, you need to be able to trust and respect that person. You need that person to be candid and informed, compassionate yet honest in his/her feedback. Working with an editor who tells you what you want to hear and does not offer substantive criticism when needed to improve your manuscript inevitably yields a pleasant friendship and a poor book. Some editors are easy to work with and others are not; some will give you honest feedback and constructive criticism and some will not; some are influential within their press and some are not; some will understand your subject matter well and some will not. It is, therefore, important that you scout out *editors* as much as presses before submitting a manuscript to a publisher.

How do you get to know acquisition editors?

～ 1. *Publisher Web pages* usually contain contact information about

103

acquisition editors and a list of the areas within which they acquire books.

~ 2. *Authors* who have worked with editors previously can be a good source of information about their expertise, personality, openness, and reliability. Beware, however, of relying too heavily on the opinion of one or a handful of authors, since circumstances particular to a project may unduly skew a perspective for better or worse. Get feedback about an acquisition editor from as large a sample of authors as possible before drawing conclusions.

~ 3. *Academic conferences* are an effective way to meet acquisition editors face-to-face and to lurk and listen to them interacting with others. If editors are not meeting with authors or getting lunch, they stay at their book displays, so repeated visits to the exhibit hall will increase your chances of running into acquisition editors. A more systematic way of meeting them is to contact the editor through e-mail before the conference and arrange a specific time to chat. For advice on making contact in that way, see below.

TIP 3: Find a press committed to a timely and informed review process. Most scholarly presses require reviews of manuscript submissions by external readers selected and commissioned by the press. If your submission is sent to reviewers, be careful. Horror stories about the review process surface frequently: tales of manuscripts that seem to vanish into a black hole, their reviews taking a year or more; and accounts of presses relying heavily on the opinions of reviewers who are not well-enough acquainted with the topic of a manuscript (such as a postcolonial studies manuscript being reviewed by a scholar whose familiarity with theory and interpretive trends fossilized in the Watergate era) or who hold a grudge against an author, his/her friends, dissertation chair, or views on identity politics. This caution is especially pertinent to Native writers. Some reviewers are racist, determined to stay in control of Native Studies, and unwilling to approve a manuscript with Native concerns.

Before sending your manuscript to presses who use external reviewers, learn as much as possible about their review process. Know what might happen to your work! Become informed in particular about the expected average length of time for reviews and the editor's criteria for selecting reviewers. Good sources of information are press Web pages, the earlier experiences of potential authors (do keep in mind that some rejected authors might offer less-than-balanced opinions), and polite but direct questions put to the acquisition editors themselves through e-mails or face-to-face conversations. Most will be happy to discuss this important aspect of publishing.

Reviews of manuscripts of reasonable length (four hundred or fewer double-spaced pages) and complexity should take approximately eight weeks. Please keep in mind that presses can exert only so much control over their reviewers' mental stability, emotional outbursts, personal lives, and schedules. Sometimes that perfect reviewer brimming with invaluable comments for your manuscript is overcommitted or dealing with real-life issues, so flexibility, graciousness, and patience are highly recommended. I know authors who have lost their temper at editors over delays in receiving reviews only to receive the following week those very readers' reports, reviews that more often than not were detailed and helpful.

Commercial presses often do not have a formal review process. Submitted manuscripts are read by the editor or the editor's assistants, and a decision can be based on their opinion of the book – even if they know nothing about the subject matter.

TIP 4: Find a press committed to timely publication of manuscripts. After you have submitted an accepted, final manuscript to a press, how long until your book will appear? It is wise to ask ahead of time about the time lag between final submission and publication because the policies and procedures for presses can vary widely on this issue. Some move a project quickly into copyediting upon its arrival; others might appear to sit on a manuscript for a long time before moving it forward into the publishing stream. As with the review process, the best sources of information are direct questions to acquisition editors through conversations or e-mails and to authors who have been through the process.

The average lapse of time between submission of a final manuscript (of reasonable length and complexity, as defined above) and publication is one year. It doesn't always happen that way, though, and there can be plenty of blame on both sides. Here are some common reasons why your manuscript might be delayed in getting published even after you have worked hard, made final revisions, and sent in the accepted manuscript.

ॐ 1. *You have missed a deadline.* At the time of contract, the acquisition editor and author agree on a tentative deadline for submission of the final manuscript. Usually that date reflects both the workload capability of the author and a time frame best serving the audience and market of the book (including the annual academic conference schedule). If you are late sending your manuscript to the acquisition editor, do not be surprised if its publication is delayed – seasonal publication slots are rapidly filled, a press's staff is always busy with new projects, and a late final manuscript submission normally cannot be accommodated easily. Try to submit your final manuscript on time. I know authors who complain bitterly about delays in publication yet were months – sometimes years – behind schedule in getting their manuscript to their press.

ॐ 2. *Your manuscript is not final.* Frequently a final manuscript cannot be moved forward into copyediting because it (a) lacks all of the permissions to use images or text, the rights of which are held by others; (b) is incomplete, missing perhaps a conclusion, dedication, bibliography, or even an image; (c) is not revised along the lines agreed on by the author and acquisition editor; or (d) is not formatted to follow the press's specifications. Do not expect a press to act quickly on your manuscript if you haven't done your part in the first place. Some time ago, a respected editor of a Native anthology consisting of twenty chapters submitted a "final" manuscript in which the chapters were formatted in different fonts and lacked consistent credit lines for authors and storytellers, few permissions had been obtained for use of the original Native stories themselves, one chapter was still being rewritten, no table of contents was supplied, and another chapter was not in electronic form and needed to be scanned. The editor was nevertheless surprised and voiced displeasure over the delays in getting the anthology published.

ॐ 3. *Your manuscript is unusually complicated.* If your book manuscript is more than four hundred double-spaced pages, contains more than twenty images, is an anthology with multiple authors, and/or is built around complex design features such as sidebars or a bilingual typescript, then more time will be needed in copyediting and design to produce the book.

∾ 4. *Your book has special marketing considerations.* Occasionally, a press will choose to postpone the publication date of a book in order to best capitalize on the schedule of relevant conferences or on anticipated sales activity. For example, your book might be delayed for a few months so that its publication will coincide more effectively with a meeting or meetings where it would be unveiled, exhibited, and sold; in other cases, a book with greater sales potential might be held so that it can be issued at the start of a sales season in order to maximize review attention and retail response. Presses are responsible for communicating such delays to authors as soon as they are known.

∾ 5. *The press is inundated with projects.* Presses perceived to be successful and prestigious continually receive, review, and accept a multitude of manuscripts in their areas of reputation and are sometimes slower getting a final manuscript published than others. Remember, such presses are continually accepting book manuscripts in your area, so it is likely that many accepted projects are queued up ahead of yours. Some authors must choose between waiting two years for their book to be issued by a press seen as reputable by their tenure committee or moving forward more quickly with a less well-known publisher.

∾ 6. *The press is understaffed.* Sometimes unexpected staff shortages will lengthen the time it takes to get your final manuscript published. For example, an acquisition editor, project editor (who oversees copyediting), or valued assistant might jump to another press, thus increasing the workload on the remaining staff; or (especially because of the current budgetary crisis in higher education) there may be mandated layoffs at a press. Such staff fluctuations inevitably impact the capacity of a press to process manuscripts in a timely manner.

How to Contact a Publisher

Once you have investigated your options thoroughly and preselected a small number of presses who will probably be interested in what you have written, it is time to contact the acquisition editors at those publishing houses on your shortlist, discuss your book manuscript with them, and, ultimately, narrow the list to a single press.

Be very polite and respect acquisition editors' time; don't badger or bore them. They are professionals who deal with dozens if not hundreds of people all of the time and try their best to give each book idea full consideration. If you start monopolizing their time as an overly eager writer or student with tedious explanations of your manuscript, they will attempt to forget about you. Five ways to contact an acquisition editor are available and listed below; their advantages and disadvantages are obvious for some and depend greatly on circumstances and personalities for others.

OPTION 1: Talk face-to-face at conferences. By far the most effective strategy for getting to know an acquisition editor and discussing your project is a face-to-face conversation at one of the annual academic conferences pertinent to the subject of your manuscript. This is the most expensive approach, since you will need to pay for travel and lodging to make this meeting possible.

Don't be shy about putting yourself forward through this direct approach – most acquisition editors travel to conferences for the explicit purpose of making their work and faces known to potential new authors. By e-mail with the editor or (in the case of larger publishing houses) editor's assistant, arrange for a time to meet and discuss your book manuscript; in your e-mail, be sure to mention the title of the manuscript and, in a very succinct sentence, describe it. Ask for a brief meeting of fifteen minutes at the press's exhibit; do not invite yourself to lunch or even a coffee break.

If you have done your research thoroughly, chances are that the editor or assistant will respond favorably to your request and you will have the opportunity to present yourself and your book project in person. It is possible (particularly with some of the larger publishers) that the press will instead ask for a proposal (see below) to be submitted to them rather than grant you an audience with the acquisition editor. Depending on what you are looking for in a press and an editor, that type of response itself may be grounds for you to write off the press from your preselected shortlist, or you may choose to go ahead and submit a proposal.

If you are scheduled to meet with an acquisition editor, here are tips for a productive conversation that won't embarrass you, irk the editor, or get in the way of your work:

✺ 1. Be on time for the meeting, and be prepared to wait a bit at a busy conference. Even if you have to wait for an editor to finish speaking with someone else, it is best for you to be instantly available when the editor is ready to give you his/her full attention.

✺ 2. Do not bring the manuscript with you. Acquisition editors do not have time to read manuscripts at conferences and, because they haul boxes of books to and from conferences, they will not look kindly on being further burdened. You can have a proposal ready (see below) to give to an editor if invited, but not a manuscript.

✺ 3. Keep the focus of the discussion on your book manuscript, not on yourself. Only talk about your experiences and background if they are directly relevant to the project or if you are invited to by the editor. Remember, a press is interested necessarily more in your written work than an oral summary of your interesting or not-so-interesting life.

✺ 4. Keep it brief and succinct, focusing on the big picture. Nervous writers and students tend to babble and drown editors in detail, elaborately summarizing each chapter of the manuscript, and impulsively delivering minute academic arguments to justify a particular position. I once saw an energetic postdoctoral student hold an acquisition editor captive for nearly an hour by waving the manuscript under his nose and subjecting him to an agonizingly detailed account of each chapter. The editor could have ended the conversation but instead politely listened and, when the student had left the booth, rolled his eyes and tossed the manuscript in the trash. Spare yourself and the acquisition editor: Simply summarize in general terms the content of the manuscript and state why such a book would matter. Supply details only if the acquisition editor asks for them.

✺ 5. Describe the current status of the manuscript as truthfully as possible – whether it is complete or still being written. If the latter, estimate when it will be available for the editor to consider.

✺ 6. Say briefly why that press would serve your work well and benefit from its inclusion on its list. Mentioning the press's connection to your work lends credibility and depth to your contact.

✺ 7. Don't be nervous but remember to be respectful. Acquisition editors need new books about as much as you desire to be published, so your conversation promises much for both parties. But also keep in mind that most editors are powerful professionals with considerable training and a specialization that resonates with but does not duplicate your own.

∾ 8. Avoid lingering. Once your conversation is concluded, leave the booth and, unless invited, don't return for the rest of the conference. The acquisition editor will be concerned with other authors and projects and will be distracted if you show up again at his/her exhibit. If you wish to purchase books at that press's exhibit, do so before your scheduled meeting and not after.

By the end of this conversation, several developments could take place. You may decide that the editor and press are not appropriate for your work, thus narrowing your list of publishers even further. The acquisition editor might invite (see below) you to submit a proposal or completed manuscript for him/her to consider; on the other hand, you may be told that your work is not of interest to the press. One frustrating conclusion for writers and students is for the acquisition editor to be mildly interested but not outright encouraging about seeing your work. In such instances, I strongly recommend that you treat the lukewarm reaction as a rejection and move on to another press.

OPTION 2: Discuss your work through e-mail. If it is not possible to meet with an acquisition editor at a conference, contact him/her by e-mail. E-mail enables fairly rapid and nonintrusive communication as well as provides a useful written record of your contact with a press. Send an e-mail of not more than one moderate-sized paragraph to the acquisition editor – briefer and to the point is always better since, as with regular letters, editors receive dozens of e-mails each day and will undoubtedly skim your correspondence. Your e-mail should follow these guidelines:

∾ 1. Address your message to the correct editor at the press; it catches their attention better and shows you've done your research and know with whom you're dealing. Avoid sending an e-mail to the generic press e-mail address.

∾ 2. Begin by stating the title of your book manuscript; a particular name will stick better in the memory of the editor.

∾ 3. Make clear the status of the manuscript – is it finished? Be honest, because if an editor asks to see a manuscript you claim is finished but then has to wait, the delay will cast doubt on your judgment and reliability. If the manuscript is not finished, when do you expect it to be completed? Let the editor know exactly what you are pitching to them.

∽ 4. Ask if the editor would be interested in looking at a proposal or the whole manuscript (if it is completed).

∽ 5. Summarize in two or three sentences the contents of the manuscript and why it should be published.

∽ 6. Tell in a sentence why that press would make a good home for your work. Show that you have done your research and know the reputation and depth of the press's list of titles in your area.

∽ 7. Mention pertinent information about yourself and provide current contact information in the concluding sentence.

Most acquisition editors or their assistants will respond to such e-mail queries within a week – sometimes the response will be an outright rejection, sometimes detailed questions will be posed about the content or status of the manuscript, and sometimes you will receive an e-mail invitation to submit a proposal or manuscript.

OPTION 3: Discuss your work through a regular letter. Some writers and students still prefer the old-fashioned method of contact: writing a formal letter to a press. I counsel against this approach, primarily because regular mail delivery is slow and most editors I know reply to e-mails before letters. However, if you are most comfortable writing a letter, then above all keep the letter short and please include the pieces of information listed above for e-mail contact. The types of responses to regular mail queries are the same as those for e-mails.

OPTION 4: Discuss your work over the telephone. A few writers and students I know feel they are most effective representing their work orally; consequently, if a face-to-face conversation at a conference is not possible, then they prefer to speak to an acquisition editor on the phone. Such unsolicited contact is very risky because acquisition editors and their assistants are always busy in meetings or with manuscripts and will likely resent being tied up on the phone – even for fifteen minutes – to discuss an unfamiliar project with an unknown author. If you absolutely need to talk on the phone about your project at this early stage, then make arrangements for a good time to call by e-mail with the acquisition editor or assistant. Do not be surprised if you are put off; many editors will not talk to potential authors over the phone.

OPTION 5: Drop by a press to discuss your work. Some writers drop by a press to speak with "an editor" when traveling through a university town. Don't do it. I know of no writer who persuaded a press to publish by visiting that publisher unexpectedly. Many presses simply will not permit walk-in appointments with their editorial staff; editors who do engage in such impromptu conversations more often than not are harried and are not giving you their full attention. Some presses even have prearranged signals among staff members for terminating drop-by visits. Don't waste their time and yours – find a better way to make contact.

How Do I Submit My Manuscript or Proposal?

After you have made contact with all of the presses on your preselected shortlist, you will have presumably received an invitation from one or more of them to submit either a proposal (in the case of fiction, a synopsis) or the whole manuscript for their consideration. An invitation to submit your work to a press, whether in proposal or manuscript form, needs to be taken seriously. At this juncture, you should know enough about the presses on your shortlist to make an informed decision about which publisher is right for you. And they know enough about you to justify inviting a submission.

Accept only one invitation at a time – do not submit proposals or manuscripts to more than one press. The acquisition staff at most presses is overworked and operating under a tight budget, and consequently can only devote its editorial resources to projects for which the press has exclusive consideration. In most cases, an acquisition editor will reject a project immediately if he/she learns that it is being looked at by another press at the same time. The exception is if that press has in its guidelines the statement, "will consider simultaneous submissions if informed." Keep in mind the "if informed" part.

Select one press and inform the others who had asked to see a proposal or manuscript that your work is currently being reviewed by a publisher. Make sure to thank them for their time and support, and let them know that you will be in touch if the status of your work changes. Most acquisition editors will be gracious when they hear the news and will appreciate your straightforward and thoughtful approach.

Submitting a Proposal

If asked to submit a proposal, strive to make it concise yet packed with detail. Write not to impress but to inform, including essential information about the book manuscript in the proposal. There is a sequence to building a proposal, which can be adapted as needed for the specifics of your work.

∾ 1. *Your curriculum vitae or résumé.* Do not pad your cv or résumé; just include the basic information about occupation, education, publications, and papers. Some publishers do not want a cv; they prefer a short narrative description of your previous publications. Be sure to follow the press's instructions as to which is preferred.

∾ 2. *Overview/summary of the project.* In not more than five double-spaced pages, describe in concise, clear language the following:

● *Content.* What is your book manuscript about? Get to the point quickly and say just what needs to be said.

● *Organization.* How does your manuscript cohere as a whole? How do the chapters connect to one another?

● *Significance and context.* Why does your manuscript need to be published? Why would anyone care to read it? How does it connect to and depart from other books on this subject?

It is very important that you present the content and significance of the work as accurately as possible. An acquisition editor needs to know exactly what is being offered. If you misrepresent the work at this early stage, sooner or later either the press or the reviewers will spot the discrepancy.

∾ 3. *Format/specifications of the project.* Provide this basic but vital information about the manuscript:

● Its length or projected length (assuming double-spaced manuscript pages, in 12-point Courier)

- The number and type of illustrations, photos, maps, tables

   ❧ 4. *Timetable.* If the book manuscript is yet finished, when will it be? If it is finished, how soon could it be sent to the press for review if an editor is interested in looking at it?

   ❧ 5. *Audience/market.* Who would read and buy this book? Please be realistic about the potential size and interest of a reading audience. Acquisition editors are experienced in such matters and can spy an exaggeration from a mile away.

   ❧ 6. *Fit with the press's list of publications.* Explain how the proposed book would fit in with the current books published by that press.

   ❧ 7. *Detailed chapter outline.* Summarize each chapter in some detail, giving one or two paragraphs for each chapter.

   ❧ 8. *Sample bibliography.* If a bibliography is to be included in your book manuscript, then provide a sample list of references to demonstrate your knowledge of the field.

   ❧ 9. *Sample chapters.* If these are available, provide one or two chapter drafts that are representative of the work as a whole.

Submitting a Fiction Synopsis

Many presses prefer to see a fiction synopsis that informs the editor about the topic, manuscript length, and the writer's credentials. If you are submitting a synopsis of a work of fiction (to a commercial publisher, usually), you must make your synopsis exciting, unique, and marketable in order to catch the acquisition editor's eye. Consider that the editor or editorial assistant at a commercial publishing house wades through thousands of queries and manuscripts each year. What makes yours special? As with grant proposals (which require discussion of an entire project in as few as three pages), you must write and rewrite until you have succinctly described your entire plot in a short space.

Many fiction writers refuse to write a synopsis, believing it ties them down to one plot and one outcome. Other writers don't like to write a synopsis because they prefer to create the story as they go along. In some cases this can be a problem if an editor accepts your idea based on one synopsis but you later change it. And even if your book is wonderful, how will any publisher know if you cannot articulate the project in a synopsis?

Submitting a Manuscript

Most publishing houses post precise instructions for submitting manuscripts on their Web pages – the number of copies to send and in which format, as well as line spacing, margin, and font requirements. Out of professional courtesy and to give your manuscript its best shot, do not deviate from the press's guidelines. Here are some tips for submitting a manuscript.

❧ 1. Presses usually prefer two hard copies of a manuscript to be submitted. They should be double-spaced, single-sided, with one-inch margins and set in 12-point Courier.

❧ 2. Don't enclose the manuscripts in Styrofoam packing material or bubble wrap; both are messy, difficult to open and dispose of, and cause irritation.

❧ 3. Make sure to send the package to the correct editor and press! One scholar I know addressed his manuscript package to the correct editor and used the correct address, but he wrote the name of a rival press on the package, as well as on the enclosed cover letter.

❧ 4. The manuscript should be accompanied by a brief cover letter to the editor in which you highlight the circumstances behind the submission – the name of the acquisition editor with whom you have had contact, where and when you discussed the manuscript, and the resulting invitation to submit the manuscript. This type of cover letter usefully reminds the busy acquisition editor about you and your book manuscript.

❧ 5. If you want the manuscript returned to you, enclose a self-addressed stamped envelope of sufficient size.

❧ 6. Take what steps you can to protect your ideas, even at this early stage. Mark copyright, with your name and date on the cover page. Don't post excerpts from your work on the Web, where they may be borrowed without proper credit. In the world of academia, many authors working on nonfiction book projects stake out their territory by publishing an essay focusing on the same project before submitting to a press. Doing so sends a message to others about your engagement with certain ideas and topics.

Waiting for Reviews

Once you submit a proposal or manuscript, be patient. The acquisition editor and sometimes other members of the editorial staff are constantly reading submissions and making comments on them, seeking reviewers and assessing their reports, and issuing contracts. Like journal editors, they are very busy and are not ignoring you on purpose. Once your materials are received at a press, the acquisition editor will first screen your materials, using three criteria:

∾ 1. *Connections* to the press's list and publishing interests

∾ 2. *Readiness* for external review, if required by press procedure

∾ 3. *Feasibility* as a publication (The project may be relevant and ready to be seen by others, but it also may not be viable as a publication without additional funds to support production costs – for example, a manuscript of two thousand pages or one that is lavishly illustrated in color.)

In-house reviews vary in duration, ranging from a few weeks to months. I recommend checking in with your acquisition editor politely every two months, alerting the editor to your growing concerns if no response has been received after four months, and then reluctantly pulling the project if an in-house review has not arrived after six months.

When you receive an in-house review, the acquisition editor or assistant will inform you of the status of your project. Three outcomes are possible:

∾ 1. Your proposal or manuscript is outright *rejected*.

∾ 2. *Revisions* are asked for and you are encouraged to resubmit. Discuss the nature of the proposed revisions with your editor. If you reach agreement about the extent and direction of revisions, and you have had a positive experience so far with the press and acquisition editor, then I recommend that you revise and resubmit to the same press. Otherwise, move on.

∾ 3. Your proposal or manuscript is sent out for *external review*.

What are reviewers looking for? Here are the questions asked of referees for the University of Nebraska Press. This report form is similar to those used by other university presses:

1. Is this manuscript a contribution to the field? How important is the subject?
2. Is the scholarship sound? Is the author thoroughly acquainted with the literature on the subject? Is the manuscript marked by scholarly objectivity?
3. Is the organization of the work sound?
4. Does the manuscript have a readable style?
5. Are the author's techniques sound – the handling of notes, system of citation, bibliography, etc.? Does the author give references when scholarly completeness and integrity require them and omit them when they are needless?
6. To what audience is the work directed? Would it serve only specialists in the field?
7. Does the work duplicate or substantially recapitulate other works? What are the competing and comparable books in the field?
8. Could this work be shortened without harm or loss? If so, please suggest what could be condensed or removed.
9. Would you want this work in your personal library?
10. What is your overall recommendation? (If none of these categories seems appropriate, please feel free to frame your recommendation in your own language.) I would
    ☐ strongly recommend contracting (this is an outstanding work)
    ☐ recommend contracting (it is a good or useful work and should be made available)
    ☐ recommend publishing only if revisions are successfully made
    ☐ not recommend publishing
11. May we reveal your name to the author?
12. If your assessment is positive and the press decides to publish this manuscript, may we cite your report in our promotion?
13. If the manuscript needs revision:
    (a) Do you think the manuscript needs extensive rewriting? Or reorganization?
    (b) Does the work merit revising?
    (c) What are your specific suggestions for revision?

Most university presses require two positive evaluations from reviewers outside of the press before they can issue a contract or request the same from their advisory board. As I mentioned earlier, we all hope that those reviewers are objective, timely, and knowledgeable. Often two reviewers read a manuscript at the same time; editors may elect, however, to send it to one reviewer instead (which they sometimes will do if a manuscript is in need of some serious revision when received). A report form with standardized questions is sent to the reviewers, and they may choose to answer those questions or follow their own format. Reviewers usually receive a very modest fee or free books from the press for their service.

Some acquisition editors will ask potential authors for a confidential list of reviewers as well as names of people who would be less than objective in their evaluations (for example, people with whom authors have had pointed personal or professional disagreements). It is the interest of your manuscript to do so, but don't submit the names of friends or others who will automatically agree with your opinions and work – a rubber-stamp review process helps no one. Editors will frequently draw one reviewer from the supplied list and select one of their own (usually your submitted list will greatly overlap with the editor's pool of reviewers anyway). I advise that if your editor doesn't raise the possibility of your supplying a list of potential reviewers that you respectfully do so.

As discussed earlier, external reviews should take around eight weeks. I suggest that you contact your acquisition editor about the status of the reviews if you haven't heard from him/her for four months; if reviews are not forthcoming by eight months, I would first alert the editor to your concerns. If a mutually agreeable solution and schedule cannot be reached, then graciously withdraw the manuscript from consideration.

Once reviews are completed, the acquisition editor or assistant will send them to you. As with the in-house review, there will be one of three outcomes.

1. The reviews are universally negative and your proposal or manuscript is rejected. The reviewers found many problems that could not be remedied. In such instances, your acquisition editor will usually recommend alternatives, such as publishing the strongest chapters as articles or revising and resubmitting to another press that might look more kindly on your work.

2. **The reviews are mixed and revisions are asked for before your project can be further considered by the press.** In such instances, reviewers have found much to admire about the concepts behind your book but feel that the present execution needs improvement. When receiving such reviews, you need to step back and not get emotional about your work – and I realize that is a difficult thing to do. Are the reviewers correct? Do they reflect what readers would say if your book was published as is? If so, then it is time to take a deep breath, roll up the sleeves, listen to the most salient of the reviewers' and acquisition editor's recommendations, revise, and resubmit. If you and the press are on the same page about revisions, I would recommend that you revise and resubmit, keeping in mind that most book manuscripts are in need of revision before a contract is issued.

3. **The reviews are overall positive, the acquisition editor and you agree to some final revisions, and then the press presents your project to its advisory board, seeking permission to offer a contract.** Please keep in mind that an advisory board does not rubber-stamp manuscripts and that projects can be rejected even at this late stage. If you have done your research, however, you will have a good sense of your chances with that press's advisory board.

What to Do If Your Proposal or Book Manuscript Is Rejected

Take several deep breaths. Don't despair. Be persistent. Presses reject 95 percent of submissions, and it happens to all of us. Truthfully. If you do not develop a thick skin and learn that rejections and criticism are a part of the business, then you'll have a tough time surviving as a writer or scholar. Stephen King tells us in his *On Writing* (Scribner, 2000) about his frustrations over finding success; Tom Clancy's *Hunt for Red October* (Naval Institute Press, 1984) was reportedly rejected by thirty publishers before being picked up by a book publisher and then made into a movie. Almost all well-known writers will claim multiple rejections as they doggedly kept writing. Believe in yourself and what you have to say.

Three of my books were initially either rejected or given strange suggestions for revision that I didn't care to take. I felt there was nothing wrong with my submissions, so I didn't give up. Not only were my book manuscripts accepted, they won awards. My *American Indian: Stereotypes and Realities* was turned down by more than twenty major presses for the same reason: They didn't believe it was marketable, claiming there "was no audience for this kind of book." Clarity International, however, took a chance and that book is now in its ninth printing as a text in U.S. and European universities. You can't take rejection personally. Sometimes publishers simply do not have an adequate grasp of your subject to assess it. Sometimes a rejection reflects as much on a press's taste as on the merits of a work. An editor friend of mine once told me of his anguish when looking through reject files at the now-famous authors that his reputable press chose not to work with.

But also be honest with yourself. If you have received consistent and constant criticisms about a project, then you absolutely need to comprehend that your manuscript or its underlying ideas have serious problems. Sift through the reviewers' comments and take their recommendations as constructively as possible. Revise and resubmit to another press on your shortlist. Be prepared to share the earlier reviews with the new press and make very clear how you have revised and improved the manuscript since then.

Question: Is There Racism in Publishing?

Many Native writers have difficulty finding a publisher. Activists maintain there is much racism in the publishing world. I agree, but many times you can find ways around it if you have researched your publishers and acquisition editors carefully. For example, my *Repatriation Reader: Who Owns Indian Remains?* (University of Nebraska Press, 2000) was initially reviewed by a "Great Lakes press" and it was rejected. Why? Two reviewers strongly recommended publication, while a third – who took an unconscionable eight months to read the anthology – gave a blistering review that criticized all the Native authors, including Vine Deloria Jr., James Riding In, and me. The essays that were anti-repatriation (and happened to be authored by white scholars) were hailed. The book was then rejected by the editor with the explanation, "Well, we've always used this reader and because he's emeritus, the editorial board gives his opinion greater weight." So there you have it. A racist anthropologist with much clout at that university had the power to reject a manuscript because of his anti-repatriation views. It was picked up by Nebraska, however, and the sales statistics reveal its popularity.

More publishers than you might suspect are uninformed about Indian Country and are unthinkingly suspicious of Native perspectives, particularly those that are unsettling and activist, written by nonreservation (that is, less recognizable) Natives, or steeped in oral traditions rather than "documented" archival research. One acquisition editor friend of mine could get provocative Native book manuscripts about current issues accepted by his director and advisory board only if he represented them as "cutting edge" rather than "radical" or "activist." Most publishers eschew working with tribal organizations, finding their decision-making processes and methods of working with outsiders maddeningly slow and indirect. Many are reluctant to publish works by nonreservation or bicultural Native writers or those from small tribes, believing (correctly, it is sad to report) that general readers gravitate to books on "recognizable" Native topics, such as religion or the "Indian Wars," or to larger communities with currency, such as the Cherokees, Lakotas, or Crows.

University and commercial presses still tend to bottleneck the evaluation process through the same old reviewers who support the racist status quo in the field of Native Studies and will not recommend publication of books that challenge their views regardless of how well the manuscripts are written. The number of complaints I continue to hear from Native writers about unfair or inappropriate reviews is stunning. Native writers and non-Natives who wish to write outside the mainstream need to spend additional time finding a publisher that appreciates and respects their work.

Consider these things if you are rejected or if you receive what you perceive to be an unfair amount of criticism:

● Pat yourself on the back because you have actually taken to time to write something and have taken the chance by submitting it for publication. Not all scholars bother to write, you know. It's too difficult and time-consuming for many.

● Keep in mind that not all reviewers are kind in spirit. Some reviewers live (and love) to criticize because they think it makes them look smarter than the person who wrote the book. Graduate students are especially concerned about looking good and they often give the most thorough reviews. (This is not necessarily the same as being mean-spirited, however. They also usually review journal articles, not book submissions.) Other reviewers are territorial and as a protective strategy will unfairly smear any book that happens to in their "territory" of study. Still others are jealous of your work and are not about to give you a passing grade. Some readers, like the anthropologist who slammed *Repatriation Reader* clearly illustrates, will uphold their deeply held ideologies and will not allow upstart Natives to voice their opinions. Some reviewers are retaliatory. They will use a reading opportunity to get back at you for giving them a poor reading in the past, for a critical book review you may have given them, or maybe because you didn't hug them at the last conference. You absolutely cannot underestimate the destructive power of territoriality, jealousy, and politics in the writing business.

● Go over the reviews carefully and make certain that the comments about incorrect dates, names, places, and other facts are accurate. If those are the main problems, you can fix them.

● Consider the advice above about finding a publisher who wants your kind of work. Critiques about methodology, however, such as the use of oral testimonies versus using only textualized data, are ideological debates. All the calm persuasive arguments to the editor about why your ideology is the right one may get you no place if you are with the wrong editor. It is especially important for junior scholars to find the right publishing house because their arguments cannot override those of the established scholars who uphold the status quo.

● Do not fail to revise when publishers have given you logical reasons why your book was rejected. I am aware of several books that were rejected by presses for specific reasons, but those books ended up being published at another press. They were written in the same manner as when submitted to the press that rejected them! Not to revise when you should (even if you find a press willing to take your book) will invite criticism from readers (oftentimes this will be in the embarrassing form of a book review in a scholarly publication or newspaper) who will reinforce what that first editor told you.

Q & A

Q: *Should I get an agent?*

A: That depends. Few students or scholars hire agents, but some writers argue that an agent is indispensable for getting represented effectively and protecting what you have written. Other writers claim that you can submit your work yourself and keep all of the royalties rather than sharing 10 or 15 percent with an agent.

For authors greatly concerned with revenue, an agent is useful for negotiating contracts. Keep in mind also that many commercial book and magazine publishers won't even glance at your query letter – much less a submission – unless it is submitted by a reputable agent. But doing so can be expensive and very difficult. In order to secure an agent you often must have published at least one successful book, have a famous author friend who can make connections, or be the author of that rare, dynamite first effort that might attract an agent. I found publishers for my first ten books but, needing to branch out to larger publishing houses, I secured an agent who proved instrumental in locating a home for one of my recent books.

Finding an agent can be an ordeal and can take as long as submitting your book manuscript and waiting for a response from a publisher. Agents naturally want to read your work since they only want to represent clients who can make them money. If your work is not marketable to a popular audience, then there is no incentive for them to waste their time on you and your manuscript. Sadly, many agents, like publishers, know little about Native peoples and assume that books about them – unless they contain a romantic or New Age slant – will not sell well.

Q: *I am Native writer of fiction. Should I submit my work to a university press?*

A: Some Native writers of fiction do not submit their work to university presses because they want to work with publishing houses that can pay them more for their work and, at the same time, they are put through a less arduous review process than with university presses. But be forewarned, only a half a handful of Native writers have found success approaching major publishing houses, mainly because of prominent agents. There are few university presses that focus on fiction, and those that do have one of two weaknesses: their fiction series is edited by one or two writers who control the list (and whose works are usually the mainstay of that list), or the press editor often knows absolutely nothing about fiction yet still decides who is worthy of giving that fiction work a critical review.

Reviewers of fiction submissions to academic presses tend to over-analyze and, true to the nature of their field, they often use incomprehensible jargon to describe your work. Quite often non-Native reviewers completely misunderstand what it is that Native writers have composed, and if you are a Native writer, you may find yourself caught in the cycle of endlessly explaining to the editor what your work means.

Even if your work is terrific, the press may not take it because of endless political protocol within the press. One notable university press that has been a major publisher of works on Natives for decades requires three positive reviews of a novel before it will even consider publishing it. If there is even one suggestion made by a reviewer that press then requires the author to revise and resubmit the work for further consideration. Keep in mind that even if your book is good, or even great, a reader can make suggestions and you will have to answer to that reader in detail as to why you agree or disagree with what he/she has written.

I submitted a novel to the university press mentioned above and all three readers strongly recommended publication. However, one reader wanted a different ending, which is, of course, a completely subjective suggestion. Because of that one suggestion, the press asked me to change the ending, which would have ruined the entire story. I wouldn't change it and withdrew my submission. Don't change your story to suit just one person.

You may want to consider copyrighting. In the world of academia, many authors who are working on nonfiction book projects inform others what they are writing about. That way others know that you are already writing about that theme. It's not quite as easy with fiction. After sending my first novel to a university press, I received positive reviews from all but one reader, one who not only made nonsensical comments but also wrote some things that clearly revealed his identity.

His review included the admission that he had just received the galleys for his latest book. Interestingly, his book emerged more than two years later, long enough for him to have made some rewrites. (A book generally appears six months after first-round galleys.) Imagine my surprise to find a good many of the exact same themes in his book that were in mine. In fact, a master's student who did his thesis comparing my work to this other writer's even made the assumption that because of the similar aspects of the novels the writer and I had probably "collaborated." (I have never met the man.) It is also significant to note that many members of my tribe say this author knows little about our tribe that he writes about – he gets his information from books. Considering that some of my ideas were quite original and bizarre and they appeared in his work, I can certainly believe it. I also have recently discovered that a reviewer of one of my novellas has lifted the entire theme of the novella for her next book. Proving all this, however, is quite impossible especially since these writers have ardent fans who would never believe they would do such a thing.

When it comes to fiction, I now always mark copyright, with my name and date on the cover page. You should, too, especially if you plan on submitting to a university press. Better yet, do not submit your fiction to a university press. I never will again.

Q: *I try to be careful in my writing and to cite sources, to check facts, and to come with unique ideas. Why do I see so many published books that are poorly written and conceptualized, have nothing new to say, and fail to include all discussions in the fields?*

A: Yes, there are many bad books on library shelves, and the reasons for this include the following: publishers believe they have an audience for that book; the book manuscript was sent to reviewers who don't have the expertise or the nerve to properly critique it and it is approved for publication; some publishers are impressed if the author has already written a few books, so they take the new manuscript without any kind of review process; the publishers do not send the book to reviewers who would properly evaluate its worth.

Way too often we see poorly written books with positive blurbs on the back cover. This disturbing trend usually has its basis in politics: the reviewers are friends of the author or the reviewers want to support the

CHAPTER TEN

The Contract and the Second Wait while Your Manuscript Becomes a Book

The Contract

Once your proposal or manuscript has been accepted, the press will want to formalize its publishing agreement with you through a contract. Upon hearing that their first submission has been accepted for publication, many writers are more interested in the pending book than the terms of their contract. But before you jump in, look carefully at and reflect on the various terms of the contract before you sign. If you have questions, feel free to ask your acquisition editor; most contracts contain standard terms and clauses and the editors are used to going over them with authors. And if you have concerns or want changes, don't be afraid to raise those points with the editor. Listen respectfully to what the editor has to say, as there may be very good reasons why a contract has certain language, terms, or clauses. If you are nervous about signing a contract, then pay a lawyer or find an agent to advise you.

There are many clauses in a contract. The most important ones have to do with the following:

～ 1. *Final or advance contract.* If a complete manuscript was reviewed and accepted, then you will be issued a final contract. If what was submitted was a proposal or an incomplete manuscript, then chances are that you are being issued an advance contract. An advance contract legally commits your project to a press, but it also requires that the finished or revised book manuscript itself be reviewed and approved (by the advisory board, if you are working with a university press). Consequently, an advance contract can be risky: if the revised or completed manuscript does not receive supportive reviews, the press doesn't have to publish. Period. It's heartening when a publisher shows good faith in you and your work by offering a contract before it is completely finished, but do keep in mind that publication is not guaranteed. The press needs to protect itself and you need to do your work, even after getting an advance contract.

∾ 2. *Deadline*. This is the date your acquisition editor expects you to turn in the final version of the manuscript (along with a disk). Be very realistic about this deadline when the contract is put together. Don't be late; the publisher usually has the right to void the contract if your final manuscript isn't submitted on time. Don't treat the deadline like that of a college or graduate school paper; extensions may not be granted. If you are delayed, however, be sure to contact your acquisition editor, explain the reason, and propose a new deadline. Nearly all editors will be understanding and allow a later date of submission.

∾ 3. *Copyright*. In theory, the person who owns the copyright of a set of materials owns the rights to reproduce it and license it to others. The copyright holder of a book is listed on the page following the title page.

Most presses by default at contract time will assign the copyright of your book manuscript to themselves or their host university (if a university press). When negotiating a contract, I recommend that you ask for the copyright to be in your name. Please remember that by doing so you will be responsible for registering and paying for the copyright. Owning the copyright to your book is largely a symbolic gesture for the life of the book at that press, since the other clauses of the contract allow the press to reproduce and license the book on your behalf. *But if the book goes out of print, having the copyright in your name becomes very important because you, not the press, will be able to seek a new publisher or sell rights to the book.*

∾ 4. *Royalties*. Every contract will contain royalty terms. The royalty is a percentage of the profit that the publisher makes from selling and licensing your book. A list royalty is a percentage of the original retail price; a net royalty is a percentage of what the publisher receives after the original retail price has been discounted to buyers like bookstores. Clearly, list royalties earn more revenue for authors, and they are usually included in contracts from commercial presses and for books from university presses that are intended to make money. If your book manuscript is scholarly, don't waste your breath asking for list royalties;

given the slump in today's academic buying market, you will be lucky to receive any royalties on the first five hundred copies sold.

Sometimes presses will offer an advance against royalties if they are optimistic about a book's sales prospects. An advance is a payment ahead of time, based on the assumption that your book will sell a certain number of copies. It's wonderful to get such a lump sum, but keep in mind that you will receive no additional royalties from your book until the advance has been paid back to the press.

Some publishers will want to buy your work outright and you will receive no royalties. If your book will sell only a modest number of copies, this option might be viable for you. On the other hand, if you feel that the book will attract a sizable audience, then you will probably want to opt out of such an offer.

∾ 5. *Subsidiary rights.* Subsidiary rights stipulate where and how a press can license your work (or parts of it) to others. Cash-strapped university presses in particular need the small but additional revenue from subsidiary rights to break even on expenses related to your book or support other scholarly books that will not turn a profit. Common subsidiary rights include foreign rights and translations, book clubs, periodicals, anthologies, electronic editions, and so-called transformational rights that include television, cinema, stage, and radio. The press will manage these rights and represent your work, and you will receive a percentage of the royalties or fees they receive for licensing.

∾ 6. *Reversion of rights.* To protect your work if it goes out of print, make sure the contract contains a clause that provides a way for you to get the rights back to your book if the press no longer publishes it. Normally the reversion process entails an author's formal request for a reversion of rights in a letter to the press. Please note that reversion of rights usually occurs only if a book is declared out of print by a press. That happens less often today. The increasing sophistication of print-on-demand technology has encouraged many university presses to extract more revenue from handfuls of sales each year by hanging onto all their titles and licensing them to print-on-demand companies.

∾ 7. *First look.* Some book contracts include a clause requiring you to submit your next book to that press so they can have the rights of "first look" and refusal. While it may seem flattering for a publisher to be interested in future work before you have even written it, in reality this clause may restrict your choices. Sadly, many authors who have had poor experiences with a press are bound contractually to send their next work to them. Furthermore, the legality of such a clause has been challenged in recent years. I advise resisting the inclusion of this clause in your book contract instead of making the mistake I did. My first fiction book was published by a press that ultimately was hugely disappointing in their lack of advertising and submitting my work to award committees. Even after the book won an award (only because I sent it out myself) the press would not advertise it as an "award winner" because it was not the National Book Award. But I was committed by contract to send them my next book. The editor I worked with continued to send me e-mails asking when my next work would arrive on her desk. On the advice of several colleagues who have successfully wiggled out of this requirement, I sent her the first draft of another book that took me all of one week to pull together. I figured the editor wouldn't even bother to send it out for review and would reject it outright. To my horror, she sent it out to reviewers who knew it was my work (because she told them) and expressed their dismay at my carelessness, lack of concern with presentation, and so on. I never dreamed that the editor would send that out, but she did and I got stuck with a reputation I don't need. Better to send in your best work then turn down their contract instead of looking foolish. Ironically, after close inspection of my contract, there was no "first look" clause. The editor had merely told me there was one (repeatedly and aggressively) and I had neglected to look myself.

Revising and Submitting the Final Manuscript

OK. The contract has been negotiated and signed. Is your hard work over? Not yet. Now it is time to roll up your sleeves, make final revisions, and send the complete manuscript back to the press.

Sound simple? It's not. In most instances, after a contract has been issued, you will receive in the mail a packet of information pertaining to the final preparation of your manuscript. The press's instructions and guidelines need to be read carefully and followed because, as I mentioned earlier, turning in an incomplete or incorrectly prepared manuscript will undoubtedly delay your book.

Before you send your final manuscript back to the press, make sure to do the following:

ᐁ 1. *Revise the manuscript properly.* By this point, you and the acquisition editor have agreed on what final changes need to be made to your manuscript before the press will move it into copyediting. Be sure to complete all of those revisions in good faith; if you sidestep important, agreed-upon changes, the acquisition editor or assistant will spot the failure and will insist that the revisions be made.

ᐁ 2. *Obtain permission to use all images and texts copyrighted by others.* If you need permission to use images or passages from texts, interviews, or stories, begin working on them as soon as possible after a contract has been issued. They can take time to track down and document, and if some permissions are missing when you submit a final manuscript, the press will hold onto your work until they arrive. Most presses send a sample permission request form with their instructional materials for you to adapt as needed.

ᐁ 3. *Submit all of the final manuscript at the same time.* Don't send parts of the manuscript and inform the editor that the rest "will arrive shortly." The press will not move your manuscript into copyediting until *all* of it is in their hands. That includes not only every component of the text but also each image or table.

ᐁ 4. *Format the manuscript properly.* Follow the press's guidelines for formatting the manuscript exactly; if you have questions or are having trouble, contact your acquisition editor. Abide by the instructions, for example, setting the type in a certain font, disembedding notes, pagination, line spacing, and providing captions for maps and illustrations.

ᐁ 5. *Send both hard and electronic copies of the manuscript.* Presses generally will want two hard copies of your final manuscript and a copy on disk. *Make sure that the hard and disk copies are exact duplicates.*

The Second Wait while the Manuscript Becomes a Book

After submitting your final manuscript, it will take on the average one year for your book to be published. I suggest that during that time you begin working on your next project. Stop watching the mailbox and get on with your life! You can sometimes complete another project by the time your book comes out in print and you can be ready to begin the process once more. The press knows its responsibilities and soon enough will be bothering you with a copyedited manuscript, galleys, book copy, and marketing matters.

Let's go through the basic steps in publishing that most affect you after a final manuscript is submitted.

෨ 1. *Establishing a final title.* As soon as possible after receiving a final manuscript, the press will firmly establish the final title of your book. It is necessary to do so at this early stage because the marketing of a forthcoming title (see below) begins as early as possible and the press needs a fixed title for purchasers and reviewers.

Titles can become a very charged issue and a frequent bone of contention between an author and a press. For the months and years that authors work on a project, they tend to identify it by a certain name and thus become wedded to a title. It can be disconcerting when an acquisition editor recommends changes to or even dropping a beloved title or subtitle. I recommend in such instances that you listen carefully to your editor, understand the rationale behind his/her recommendation – remember you chose to work with this person because of his/her experience in such matters – and then respond in a measured and cooperative manner. Learn from each other and find common ground for a title. In most cases, the press and author will come to a mutually agreeable solution; if not, the press has the final say over the title of your book unless the contract says otherwise.

෨ 2. *Copyediting.* After your manuscript is checked for completeness, permissions, format, and adherence to agreed-upon revisions, it will be moved into another editorial department run by a managing editor. This department is the intermediary between acquisitions and production, the acquiring and designing of your book; its main task is to get into the fine details of a manuscript and prepare it thoroughly for the production department.

Your manuscript will first be copyedited, a crucial job undertaken usually by a freelance copyeditor outside of the press who is overseen by a project editor on the managing editor's staff. The copyeditor will go through the manuscript carefully, making recommendations for stylistic improvements and format consistency to the work in order to enhance clarity and readability and ensure conformity to accepted guidelines for your type of publication (such as adhering to the conventional way to render anthropology citations for an anthropology manuscript). Most such changes today are done electronically on a disk copy of your manuscript.

You will receive the copyedited manuscript and have the right to approve all changes. The copyedited manuscript will have all sorts of copyeditor's marks on it; specific questions about content to you are usually put at the bottom or on the margins of the pages. You are expected to read the copyedited manuscript carefully and expeditiously, and answer all of the copyeditor's questions. Any delay on your part may affect the publication date of the book.

᠁ 3. *Reviewing page proofs.* The manuscript is then sent to a typesetter who, using the copyedited manuscript that you have seen and approved, creates pages that look like a book, in proper order with page numbers. With the interior design taking shape, only a very few changes are permitted and possible at this late point in the process. According to most contracts, you will be charged for each alteration to the page proofs if the changes are many.

᠁ 4. *Creating an index.* Once you receive your page proofs, it is your turn to make your final contribution – the index of people, places, and concepts that will appear at the end of the book. Some books such as fiction do not need an index, but if you need one, only a few weeks are permitted to create it. Some writers prefer to hire someone to do it for them, which currently costs about three dollars per indexed book page. If you prefer to tackle the tedious but not difficult job yourself, here are some tips:

Read through the manuscript and write each term, name, place, and concept at the top of a 3 x 5 card.

Write down the book page numbers where the term appears on the 3 x 5 card.

Make piles of cards in alphabetical order, grouping each letter in a separate pile (all the As in one pile, the Bs in the next, and so forth). This method will allow you to quickly find the card for a particular index term, and the cards can be put away in order so you can continue your indexing the next day. You will need a lot of cards and much space to do the work.

When you're finished listing all relevant page numbers on the cards, type the index terms and corresponding page numbers into a single long list and send it to the press.

∾ 4. *Creating the cover.* A cover will be designed sometime around the middle of the process. I know that a cover design sometimes matters greatly to authors. You can make suggestions about the cover, but the publisher has the final say. The design unit of the publishing house understands that the cover can sell copies and attract attention to a book, so they spend a great deal of time and effort designing the most eye-catching, effective, and appropriate cover they can. You can ask to see the result, and if you think the cover is truly horrid, tell the press exactly why it is wrong for your book.

To minimize such heartbreak, I suggest that at contract time you come up with multiple suggestions for a cover to share with your acquisition editor, who will represent your interests at the press. This way you will not become too attached to one image or another and can enable the design team to draw from a pool of your ideas. If you do not have an idea for a cover, then stay out of it and focus on more important matters such as the copyedited manuscript and index.

∾ 5. *Marketing.* The press works on behalf of your book in several ways to promote and call attention to it through advertising and direct mail, review media, awards, exhibits and program brochures at conferences, and the press's various catalogs and Web site. Here's a rundown of some useful points to remember about marketing.

∾ *Author information form.* University presses and other publishers send out long forms to authors at the time of contract in order to gather basic information about you and your book; that information is very important and will be used in their marketing plans. The types of information they will ask for include possible awards that your book would qualify for (be realistic), suggestions for places to advertise and get your book reviewed, and a brief synopsis of the book, which will be consulted when creating the cover copy (see below) and ads.

∾ *Catalogs.* When your book is published, it will appear once in the seasonal catalog of a press, which is issued twice a year (spring/summer and fall/winter) and contains a detailed listing of all of the new books published during that time. Your book might also appear continually in subject catalogs, which group the press's offerings by general similarity of topic or field of scholarship (such as Native Studies, translations, sports, etc.).

∾ *Copy.* A concise, usually punchy description of your book will appear on the cover and in catalogs. The main objective of copy is to intrigue readers and call attention to your book; describing content is secondary. A preliminary draft of your book's copy is prepared, usually by the acquisition editor, when the final manuscript is received. For copy, the editor will draw on his/her intimate knowledge of the book manuscript as well as information you have supplied in the author information form. The marketing staff will make some adjustments to the copy and send it to you for approval.

∾ *Awards.* Most presses maintain and constantly update preexisting lists of awards relevant for your type of book, and they will fill out the paperwork and send in books themselves to the award committees. Nonetheless, there are always new awards or ones that they missed; it is up to you to let them know of such possibilities.

∾ *Conferences.* As with awards, presses are already familiar with the major annual conferences that are best for exhibiting and selling your book. If you know of special, one-time conferences that are appropriate for your work, let them know. In most cases, the marketing staff will be happy to send books and/or order forms.

∾ *Book signings and interviews.* Commercial presses routinely sponsor book signings and author interviews as part of their national marketing outreach. The tight budgets of most university presses don't permit them to do so, though they are willing and ready to send books to signings (such as at local bookstores) that you have helped arrange.

Q & A

Q: *My publisher doesn't market my book very well. How can I help?*

A: There is nothing wrong with self-promotion. How do you think some people you know get prestigious jobs? Politics and schmoozing account for many appointments. If you wish to support your publisher's marketing efforts or feel that they are not making a sufficient effort to publicize your book, then I recommend doing a little honest politicking yourself and create a Web page containing information about your book. Connect your page through keywords to search engines and provide a link to your press's page so interested buyers can deal directly with the purchasing department. If you're a Native writer, contact site masters at Native pages such as http://www.hanksville.org/NAresources/ and ask if they will add your name and Web page link to their page.

Creating Your Curriculum Vitae and Résumé

Now you have a few publications under your belt, some book reviews, conference presentations, and some committee work. Or, you're not a student and have some writings you'd like to put into some kind of compilation. How should you present your work so others can learn what you have accomplished?

I've served on seven search committees, have sat on numerous grant and fellowship deliberation committees, and have seen more than a few cvs (curricula vitae) and résumés. Some are clear and informative while others are meant to deceive or they come across as deceptive. You do not want your cv to fall into the latter two categories.

These are the obvious things to keep in mind:
● Be honest about your job and publication histories. If readers have a question about how you have presented either, they will find out the truth. All it takes is few phone calls. Native Studies may be a large field, but it is not an enormous field. People in this area have networks and they know much about what has been published. You may be able to explain your error or embellishment, but if you have made an obvious attempt to deceive, by the time readers become suspicious it'll be too late.
● Organize your résumé into a logical, easy-to-read format.
● Do not write hazy descriptions about accomplishments in an attempt to convince readers you've done more than you really have.
● Readers can tell when you're fibbing.
● Readers can tell when you're desperate to stretch a skimpy record.
● Always include volumes and page numbers of your publications.

A Sample Résumé Dissected

Here is a basic résumé outline. I use excerpts from my CV as an example. This is the result of eighteen years of work. Younger scholars and writers just getting started may not have as much, but they can use the same format.

Curriculum Vitae

Devon Abbott Mihesuah[1]
Professor of Applied Indigenous Studies and History
College of Social and Behavioral Science
P.O. Box 15020
Northern Arizona University, Flagstaff AZ 86011–5020
e-mail: devon.mihesuah@nau.edu
Web site: http://jan.ucc.nau.edu/ mihesuah
Tribal Enrollment: Choctaw Nation of Oklahoma[2]

EDUCATION[3]

Ph.D. (May 1989): History, Texas Christian University
Major Field: American History
Minor Fields: Colonial Latin America; Spanish Borderlands
Dissertation: "History of the Cherokee Female Seminary: 1851–1909."
  (Won Phi Alpha Theta/Westerners International Award for Best Dissertation in Western History. Directed by Donald E. Worcester)[4]
M.A. (May 1986): History, TCU

---

1. Do not put your title before your name since you list it below.

2. If you are not tribally enrolled, do not write anything about a tribe. You do not need to include your date of birth, number of children, and health status. This is not information that interviewers can ask you anyway. It's not anyone's business, so leave it off unless you are compelled to tell readers about yourself.

3. This is a section where some writers get into trouble. Put the degree, your major and minor, the date you received it and where. You must be specific. If any of these aspects are not clear, then you will be immediately suspect.

4. If you won a major award for something you wrote in graduate school, you can put it here, but leave fellowships and grants for the category below.

M.ED. (May 1982): Secondary Education/Biology/Physics, TCU
B.S. (May 1981): Secondary Education/Biology/Physics, TCU

PROFESSIONAL EXPERIENCE[5]

Professor of Applied Indigenous Studies and History, Northern Arizona University, Flagstaff (College of Social and Behavioral Science): 2000–. The "Mountain Campus" has 13,400 undergraduate and graduate students, including 1,400 Native students, the second largest in the country.[6]
Search Committee, College Dean
Search Committee, Department Chair
Search Committee, Recruitment Officer, Applied Indigenous Studies and Forestry
Professor of History, NAU (College of Arts and Sciences): 1999–
Associate Professor of History: 1995–99
Assistant Professor of History: 1989–95
Duties included:
Western Historian and Chicano/a Historian search committees
Departmental Committee on Faculty Status
Chair, Native American Studies Minor
Chair, Indian Historian search committee
University Faculty Senate
Institutional Review Board for the Protection of Human Subjects in Research
Chair, Native American Research Guidelines Committee
Departmental Graduate Committee
President's Native American Program Council
Presidential Ambassadors for Cultural Diversity

5. Highlight each position. You do not have to list duties like I have here. Paragraph descriptors are not necessary. You may have been a lifeguard and babysitter, but unless it pertains to the job you are applying for and you have absolutely nothing else to put in this category, leave those jobs off.
6. I put a short descriptor about NAU mainly because most people have no idea where it is or that it has a large student enrollment. The number of Natives enrolled is also pertinent because of my area of study and what I teach.

History Dept. Research and Undergraduate Curriculum Committees

OTHER EXPERIENCE

Editor, *American Indian Quarterly*: 1998–

Associate Editor of History, *American Indian Quarterly*: 1993–98[7]

Editor, University of Nebraska Press Book Series: Contemporary American Indian Issues, 2000–2005. See Peter Monoghan, "Challenging the Status Quo in Native American Studies." *Chronicle of Higher Education*, January 17, 2003,
http://chronicle.com/weekly/v49/i19/19a01601.htm[8]

Board of Trustees, Museum of Northern Arizona, 1999–2001
Executive Committee, MNA
Chair, Research and Acquisitions Committee, MNA

Women of the West Museum Project, Boulder co: 1992–93. Consultant, Exhibit Content Development Project at the Women of the West Museum: 1994–96[9]

Consultant, "Edge of the Rez," an *Arizona Daily Sun* (Flagstaff) and KNAU radio series on Bordertown Race Relations: 1996

Consultant to the Texas Indian Commission's and Texas Historical Commission's Committee on the Acquisition and Disposition of Human Remains and Sacred Objects: 1984–89

Consultant to Northeastern State University's Archives and Special Collections: 1988–89

Panelist, NEH Public Humanities Projects: 1992

---

7. Note that there is a distinction between "editor" and "associate editor." If you are an associate editor of a journal, do not list yourself as editor. I received a call last year from someone out of state asking about a candidate for a position at her university. The person listed "editor" on her cv. I knew that she had only served in an assistant capacity. This may have been an oversight on her part, but it comes across as deceptive. Be specific.

8. If you have an essay that is easily accessible on the Web and pertains to what is on the list, you can slip that in, such as the *Chronicle* piece.

9. Once you are no longer serving on a committee or project, you need to document when you stopped. Leaving the dates open-ended is misleading.

Consultant, NEH Interpretive Research Programs/Collaborative Projects: 1992

Consultant and Reviewer, *Western Social Science Journal, American Indian Culture and Research Journal, Choice, The Historian, Frontiers, Signs*: 1990–[10]

Teaching Assistant, Department of History, TCU: 1985–88

Departmental Assistant, Department of History, TCU: 1984–85

Board Member, American Indian Center of Dallas TX: 1984–87

Computer Instructor, Upward Bound Program, TCU: 1980, 1985–86

Biology and Physics Instructor; Coach; Western Hills High School, Ft. Worth TX: 1984

Biology and Physics Instructor; Coach; Grants High School, NM: 1982–84

Supervisor, Outreach Minority Programs, Girl Scouts of America, Ft. Worth TX: 1982

Graduate Assistant, School of Education, TCU: 1981–82

Secretary, American Indian Center of Ft. Worth TX: 1977–78[11]

INDIVIDUAL ACADEMIC HONORS, GRANTS, AWARDS[12]

2004: Crystal Eagle American Indian Leadership Award, presented by the Indigenous Nations Studies at the University of Kansas

Oklahoma Writers' Federation Trophy Award for Best Nonfiction Book of 2003: *American Indigenous Women: Decolonization, Empowerment, Activism*, and Best Young Adult Novel: *Lost and Found*

2001: Wordcrafter Circle of Native Writers' Journal Editing Award for the *American Indian Quarterly*

---

10. An open-ended date means you are still doing whatever you have listed.

11. While I could elaborate on the above nine positions, they really have nothing to do with my current job or a potential position. Teaching physics has little connection with teaching Indigenous history. Simple listing tells readers you have this experience; if they want more details they can ask you.

12. This is an important section, but don't rub it in with more details than simply listing. You can put all honors, awards, and fellowships into the same list for a particular year.

2000: Oklahoma Writers' Federation Trophy Award for Best Fiction
Book of 2000: *The Roads of My Relations*[13]

1999: Critics' Choice Award of the American Educational Studies Association for *Natives and Academics: Researching and Writing about American Indians*

1996–97: Ford Foundation Postdoctoral Fellowship[14]

American Association of University Women American Postdoctoral
Fellowship (declined)[15]

NAU Organized Research Grant[16]

First prize for *Flagstaff Live!* First Annual Short Story Contest[17]

1995: Critics' Choice Award of the American Educational Studies Association for *Cultivating the Rosebuds: The Education of Women at the Cherokee Female Seminary, 1851–1909*

D'Arcy McNickle Center for the Study of the American Indian at the Newberry Library, "Indian Voices in the Academy" seminar: "The Construction of Gender and the Experience of Women in American Indian Societies: An Historical Perspective" (declined)

NAU Organized Research Grant

NAU Instructional and Curricular Development Grant

1994: Native American Students United Award for Outstanding Faculty

NAU Organized Research Grant

1993: NAU President's Award for Outstanding Faculty

NAU Organized Research Grant

Arizona Humanities Council Studies Grant

1992–93: American Council of Learned Societies Fellowship

1992: American Historical Association Albert Beveridge Research Grant

13. Book awards can also be listed next to the book in the publications list.

14. Some people like to list the amount of the award. On the other hand, many readers are already familiar with the general figures for these kinds of grants, so leave the amount out unless it's impressive.

15. Some people argue that if you receive a grant but turn it down that you should not list it. I think that if you won it, there is reason to list it!

16. I have seen cvs that list what the project was. You can do this if you don't have a lot to list on your cv as a whole. Otherwise, it is not necessary to go into detail. Grant applications, however, will require you to list topics and amounts in your cv.

17. You could write what the award was for, but you also can list it next to the publication in the list below. If it's a big award list it twice.

National Endowment for the Humanities Travel to Collections Grant

NAU Outstanding Faculty Woman of the Year Award

NAU Organized Research Grant

1990: Smithsonian Institution American Indian Community Scholar Internship

American Council of Learned Societies Travel Grant to Australia

NAU Organized Research Grant

1989: Phi Alpha Theta and Westerners International Award for Best Dissertation in Western History

1988–89: Ford Foundation/National Research Council Dissertation Fellowship[18]

1988: Texas Regional Phi Alpha Theta Award for paper, "An Ounce of Prevention: Health Care at the Cherokee Female Seminary, 1876–1909"

Newberry Library Conference, "Overcoming Economic Dependency." Travel.[19]

1987: TCU Barnett Scholar Award for Outstanding Female History Graduate Student

1986–88: Teaching Assistantship, Department of History, TCU[20]

1984–86: Departmental Assistantship, Department of History, TCU

1981–82: Graduate Assistantship, School of Education, TCU

UNIVERSITY COURSES TAUGHT[21]

U.S. History to 1877

18. Some young scholars who have applied for this award but did not get it list "finalist." If you have a skimpy cv you can list your "finalist" status, but once your career starts fleshing out, do not list the grants you did not receive. It isn't always impressive, especially if the cv readers see before yours reveals a "winner."

19. Winning "travel funds" isn't a whole lot, but it shows that you not only attended the conference, you took the time to apply for funding.

20. Job descriptions of your assistantship are not necessary unless you have not had other positions. Once you become a "part of the industry," you can omit grad school duties.

21. Listing here is adequate and pretty much self-explanatory. Do not attach course syllabi or student evaluations. Once you apply for a job, then you follow the instructions for that job description. Do not list course numbers because readers won't know what you're talking about.

U.S. History since 1877
American Indian History Survey
Introduction to Applied Indigenous Studies
Roots of Federal Indian Policy
American Indian Expressions (literary criticism and creative writing)
American Indian/White Relations to 1865
American Indian/White Relations since 1865
Honors: American Indian History to 1865
Senior Seminar in American History (Theory and Methodology of
  Writing American Indian History)
Applied Indigenous Studies: Research Methodologies[22]
"Other Americans": Race and Ethnicity in the U.S.
Graduate Readings in American History
Graduate Readings in American Indian History: Contact to 1850
Graduate Readings in American Indian History: Since 1850
Graduate Topics: American Indians since Reconstruction
Graduate Topics: American Indian Women and Colonial Domina-
  tion[23]

ORGANIZATIONS AND COMMITTEES[24]

American Indian and Alaskan Native Professors' Association
Oklahoma Writers' Federation
Phi Alpha Theta

PUBLICATIONS

BOOKS:

*Recovering Our Ancestors' Gardens: Indigenous Recipes and Guide to
Diet and Fitness.* Lincoln: University of Nebraska Press, 2005.

22. Like the senior seminar and honors courses above, you need to provide a bit
of detail sometimes so we know what you taught.
23. Be sure to differentiate between undergraduate and graduate courses like the
ones listed here.
24. Listing for this category is adequate. Younger scholars should belong to as
many as they can afford. As you mature as a scholar and gain confidence, you can
pick and choose organizations according to your needs and what works for you.

So You Want to Write about American Indians: A Guide for Scholars, Students, and Writers. Lincoln: University of Nebraska Press, 2005.[25]

With Angela Wilson. *Indigenizing the Academy: Native Academics Sharpening the Edge.* Lincoln: University of Nebraska Press, 2004.[26]

Lost and Found (novel). Forthcoming. Winner of the Oklahoma Writers' Federation Trophy Award for Best Young Adult Novel of 2003.[27]

The Lightning Shrikes (novel). Guilford CT: Lyons Press, 2003.

American Indigenous Women: Decolonization, Empowerment, Activism. Lincoln: University of Nebraska Press, 2003. Winner of the Oklahoma Writers' Federation Trophy Award for the Best Nonfiction Book of 2003.

"First to Fight": Henry Mihesuah NU MUU NU (Comanche). Lincoln: University of Nebraska Press, 2002.

Ed. *Repatriation Reader: Who Owns Indian Remains?* Lincoln: University of Nebraska Press, 2000.[28]

The Roads of My Relations (Tucson: University of Arizona Press Sun Tracks Series, 2000). Winner of the Oklahoma Writers' Federation Trophy Award for the Best Fiction Book of 2000.[29]

Ed. *Natives and Academics: Researching and Writing about American Indians.* Lincoln: University of Nebraska Press, 1998. Recipient of 1999 Critics' Choice Award of the American Educational Studies Association.

25. This is the way to list a book that has been published. I have, however, seen cvs in which the author lists a book under contract in this fashion, but the book is not yet finished nor has it been accepted. It is highly deceptive to try and give the impression that the book is out when it has in fact not even left your printer. Also, "under contract" does not mean that it has been accepted. Contracts can be broken if the work is not adequate.

26. Because I had a coeditor for the above volume, I list her name. Do not leave out your coworker!

27. Notice that the above book is not out yet, but because I put "forthcoming," readers know it is accepted, in the publishing process.

28. Note the "Ed." at the beginning of this citation. Don't try to get away with not telling that you edited a book; editing is not the same as writing the entire thing yourself.

29. It is appropriate to duplicate awards won from the awards section.

American Indians: Stereotypes and Realities. Atlanta and Regina, Canada: Clarity International, 1996.

Cultivating the Rosebuds: The Education of Women at the Cherokee Female Seminary, 1851–1909. Urbana: University of Illinois Press, 1993. Reprint, 1997. Recipient of 1995 Critics' Choice Award of the American Educational Studies Association.

CURRENTLY UNDER REVIEW:[30]
Room of Secrets
Statement of Expectations

SCREENPLAYS:
The Lighting Shrikes
The Swamp

IN PROGRESS:

Decolonization 101: Strategies for Empowerment (essays on curriculums, political involvement, and inspiring historical Native individuals such as Silon Lewis)[31]

Refereed Journal Articles and Chapters in Books:[32]

"Should 'American Indian History' Remain a Field of Study?" and "Academic Gatekeeping." In *Indigenizing the Academy*, ed. Mihesuah and Wilson. Lincoln: University of Nebraska Press, 2003.

"Anna Mae Pictou-Aquash: An American Indian Activist." In *Sifters: Native Women's Lives*, ed. Theda Perdue, 204–22. New York: Oxford University Press, 2001.[33]

30. Note this subheading. It shows that you have completed a manuscript and are in the process as far as the review.

31. "In progress" is just that. It is not "in press" or "forthcoming." There is no guarantee that you'll complete this project, but it shows that you are working on it. Keep this kind of work in a separate category.

32. This is a specific heading for "refereed" essays, not for essays that were not reviewed.

33. The more information you can supply about a piece, the better. Give page numbers so interested readers can find it if they want to. Many search committees also need to see how long the essay is. Note that you do not need to list your name as the author since we know this is your cv. Some writers in fields such as education, social work, and science, however, often collaborate with others and it is a good idea to list their names.

"American Indian Women at the Millennium." *Signs* 25:4 (2000): 1247–52.

"American Indian Identities: Comment on Issues of Individual Choices and Development." *American Indian Culture and Research Journal* 22:2 (1998): 193–226. Reprinted in *Contemporary Native American Cultural Issues*, ed. Johnson and Champagne. Walnut Creek CA: Alta Mira Press, 1999.[34]

"Indians in Arizona." In *Politics and Public Policy in Arizona*, 91–102. New York: Praeger, 1993. Reprint 1997.[35]

"Commonalty of Difference: American Indian Women in History." *American Indian Quarterly* 20:1 (1996): 15–27.

"Voices, Interpretations, and the 'New Indian History': Comment on the *American Indian Quarterly*'s special issue on 'Writing about American Indians.'" *American Indian Quarterly* 20:1 (1996): 93–109.

Editor, *American Indian Quarterly*'s special issue: "Writing about (Writing about) American Indians." *American Indian Quarterly* 20:1 (1996).[36]

"Introduction to the *American Indian Quarterly*'s special issue: The Repatriation of American Indian Skeletal Remains and Sacred Cultural Objects: An Interdisciplinary Anthology." *American Indian Quarterly* 20:2 (1996): 153–64.

"American Indians, Anthropologists, Pot Hunters, and Repatriation: Ethical, Religious, and Philosophical Differences." *American Indian Quarterly* 20:2 (1996): 229–37. Reprinted in (unauthorized) revised form as "Studying Indian Remains Violates Native Americans' Beliefs." In *Native American Rights: Current Controversies*, 26–33. San Diego: Greenhaven Press, 1998.

"'Let us strive earnestly to value education aright': Cherokee Female Seminarians as Leaders of a Changing Culture." In *Nineteenth-Century Women Learn to Write: Past Cultures and Practices of Literacy*, 103–19. Charlottesville: University Press of Virginia, 1995.

"Research Guidelines for Institutions with Scholars Who Study Amer-

34. If a piece appears in more than one book or anthology you can put them together in a cluster instead of separate listings.

35. You can list "reprint" because it shows that the work was marketable.

36. Actually, this entire issue was refereed, but since I was the editor, I don't want people to think that was not the case.

ican Indians." *American Indian Culture and Research Journal* 17 (fall 1993): 131–39.

"Out of the Graves of the Polluted Debauches: The Boys of the Cherokee Male Seminary." *American Indian Quarterly* 15 (fall 1991): 503–21.

"Despoiling and Desecration of American Indian Property and Possessions." *National Forum* (spring 1991): 15–18. Reprinted in *The Four Directions* (spring 1992): 86–89.

" 'Too Dark to Be Angels': The Class System among the Cherokees at the Female Seminary." *American Indian Culture and Research Journal* 15 (1991): 29–52.

" 'Gentleman' Tom Abbott: Middleweight Champion of the Southwest." *Chronicles of Oklahoma* 68 (spring 1990): 426–37.

"Ann Florence Wilson: Matriarch of the Cherokee Female Seminary." *Chronicles of Oklahoma* 67 (winter 1989–90): 426–37.

"Medicine for the Rosebuds: Health Care at the Cherokee Female Seminary, 1876–1909." *American Indian Culture and Research Journal* 12 (1988): 59–71.

" 'Commendable Progress': Acculturation at the Cherokee Female Seminary." *American Indian Quarterly* 11 (summer 1987): 187–201.

FICTION:[37]

"Medicine Woman." *Red Ink* 6 (spring 1998): 40–49.

"The Tamfuller Man." *Flagstaff Live!* 3 (April 17–30, 1997): 25–26. Won the *Flagstaff Live!* short story contest.

OTHER PUBLICATIONS AND PROJECTS:[38]

Comment: "Finding Empowerment through Writing and Reading or, Why Am I Doing This?: An Unpopular Writer's Comments about

37. Fiction is not nonfiction and I think the work needs to be in different categories.

38. This is for work that was not refereed. Granted, the editor read and approved it, but in the scholarly world, there is a clear distinction between refereed and not refereed. It makes all the difference in a tenure and promotion decision. Informed readers also appreciate that you are trying to be honest by separating them. By putting them all into one category, you are stating that they all were refereed when that is not the case. You know what that means. Many applicants for positions that I screened tried this and they did not succeed.

the State of American Indian Literary Criticism." For special issue titled "Empowerment through American Indian Literature," ed. Daniel Heath Justice. *American Indian Quarterly* 28:1/2 (Winter–Spring 2004): 97–102.

Editorial Comment: "Imparting Basic Empowering and Nation-Building Strategies in the Classroom." *American Indian Quarterly* 27:1/2 (winter–spring 2003): 459–78.

Comment: "Activism vs. Apathy: The Price We Pay for Both." For special issue titled "Problems in the Ivory Tower." *American Indian Quarterly* 27:1/2 (2003): 325–32.

Editorial Comment: "Decolonizing Our Diets by Recovering Our Ancestors' Gardens." *American Indian Quarterly* 27:3/4 (2003): 807–39.

Review commentary of "Indian Girls." *HEArt* 5:1 (fall 2000): 18–20.

"Interview with Denise Maloney-Pictou and Deborah Maloney-Pictou." *American Indian Quarterly* 24:2 (2000): 264–78.

"Infatuation Is Not Enough: Review of Ian Frazier's *On the Rez.*" *American Indian Quarterly* 24:2 (spring 2000): 283–86.

Editor, *American Indian Quarterly*'s special issue: "Repatriation of American Indian Skeletal Remains and Sacred Cultural Objects." *American Indian Quarterly* 20:2 (1996).[39]

"The Creek Indians." In *The Encyclopedia of the U.S.: Past and Present.* Academic International Press, 1993.[40]

"Historical Perspectives on Cultural Diversity: American Indians." *Arizona School Boards Association Journal* 24 (spring 1994): 18–22.

"Eliza Missouri Bushyhead Alberty," "Anna Mae Aquash," "Isabelle Cobb," "Rachel Caroline Eaton." In *Directory of Minority Women: Native American Women.* New York: Garland, 1993.

"American Indian Women." Paper presented at the American Historical Assn. Annual Conference. Printed in *Bulletin of the Conference Group on Women's History* 23 (May–June 1992): 18–21.

39. While this above special issue was not refereed, the subsequent book anthology based on the same essays was. It was, in fact, heavily scrutinized. I'm not sure how to explain that, but because I have many other books, I'm not going to worry about it.

40. Many young scholars put encyclopedia articles in the same section as other works. Although these kinds of writings can be the mainstay of beginning writers, it is a good idea to separate them from longer works.

"The Cherokee Seminaries." In *Encyclopedia of the American West.* New York: Macmillan, ca. 1989.[41]

"An American Success Story: The Cherokee Female Seminary." *True West* 36 (June 1989): 42–47.

Identified and captioned 100 photographs, paintings, and blueprints for the Cherokee Nation's April 12, 1989, celebration of the 100th anniversary of the opening of Seminary Hall, Tahlequah OK. Now a permanent collection at Northeastern State University.[42]

"American Indian Burial Gravesite Desecration in Texas." *Akwesasne Notes* 18 (spring 1986): 11.

"Ancestry Sacrificed to Greed." *TCU Daily Skiff,* April 24, 1985, p. 2.

BOOK REVIEWS (22 in scholarly journals)[43]

American Indian Quarterly
American Historical Review
Journal of American Ethnic History
Journal of the West
Western History Quarterly
Journal of American History
New Mexico Historical Review
Choice
Chronicles of Oklahoma

41. As with a few other entries in this category, I have somehow lost track of the page numbers. They are minor writings, however, and since there is enough here I won't worry about it. Beginning writers need to keep closer tabs on page numbers.

42. Perhaps the above could go under jobs, except that I was not paid even though it was a huge undertaking. Much research was done so I put it here.

43. Beginning scholars (and those who have been in the business for years but don't write much) tend to include the entire book review citation. Once you have fifteen reviews or many other publications (in addition to a few reviews) you do not need to list the whole review citation. It looks almost desperate to elaborate on a review.

PRESENTATIONS AND CONFERENCE PARTICIPATION[44]

2004: Interview on NPR 90.9 WBUR Boston, *Only a Game*, talk show. (*The Lightning Shrikes*)
Interview on *Native America Calling*. KUYI 88.1 FM. (*American Indigenous Women*)
Invited speaker, University of Victoria Indigenous Governance Program. "Academic Activism."
Berger Lecture, "On Becoming an Indigenous Intellectual Activist." University of Montana, Missoula, September.
Plenary speaker: "Working in and Responding to Volatile Times." Social Science Research Council/Andrew W. Mellon Foundation Summer Conference, Washington University, St. Louis.
Acceptance speech for the Crystal Eagle American Indian Leadership Award, presented by Indigenous Nations Studies, University of Kansas.
2003: Keynote speaker, "Indigenizing the Curriculum." Distinguished American Indian Speaker's Series and Workshops, University of Idaho American Indian Studies Program, November.
Interview, "Indigenous Women and Ways to Empowerment." Channel Two News (Flagstaff) weekly series on Native Issues.
2002: Invited speaker, Arizona State University Department of History, "The Importance of Indigenous Histories," December.
"Stereotypes of Native Peoples." Channel Two News (Flagstaff) weekly series on Native Issues, October.
2001: Session chair on Kennewick Man and roundtable discussant for Perdue's *Sifters*, both at Ethnohistory, Tucson, October.
Keynote speaker, "American Indians as Scholar/Activists in Indian Studies Programs." First Annual Graduate Student Conference on American Indian Research, Arizona State University, February.

---

44. Speaking is an important aspect of your career. List when, where, and the purpose of your presentation. Designate what type of speaker you were. Keynote? Invited? "Speaker" is different from "conference participant" – for the latter, you went on your own accord and were not necessarily invited or paid. There is no place to put the invitations you have; in 2003–2004, I received fifty invitations to speak but only accepted these. You can explain your other invitations in a cover letter.

Session facilitator, NEH Institute on American Indian Literature, NAU, June.[45]

Guest speaker, "American Indian Women Activists in Higher Education." American Association of University Women, Flagstaff, September.

2000: Keynote speaker at University of Utah's Native American Heritage Week Celebration, April.

Guest speaker, "American Indian Studies and Changing Methodologies of Teaching and Writing." Ball State University, September.

Guest on *Native America Calling*, November 29, 2000, http://www. nativecalling.org.

1999: Invited lecturer, "American Indian Women, Feminists, and Native Voices." University of Arizona American Indian Studies Speaker Series.

Guest speaker, "The Need to Teach, the Freedom to Learn." NAU's Faculty Senate's Speaker Series, "Fearless Learning."

Guest speaker, "American Indians and Publishing." NAU's Student Services Speaker Series.[46]

1994: Commenter, "Indian Women: Their Voices Their History," Western History Association Annual Conference, Albuquerque.[47]

Keynote speaker, "American Indian Women as Chroniclers of Their Histories." "Native Women Historians: Challenges and Issues" conference, Southwest State University, Marshall MN.

Guest lecturer, "Gender and American Indian History." "American Indians: The 21st Century" graduate studies institute, "The New West" symposium, University of Northern Colorado, Greeley.

Invited lecturer, "The New American Indian History," and Colorado

---

45. A "facilitator" is usually not a person who gives a formal presentation. However, he/she must know the topic and is the one who controls the dialogue. It is an authoritative position and should be listed here.

46. Some scholars don't list speaking engagements at their home institution, while others make "brownbag" talks the mainstays of their career. If you have a lot to list, you can easily omit "home talk," unless you are invited by the recipient of large grant.

47. A "commenter" is not the same as a "speaker," but he/she has to know about the subject matter of the session. The commenter has to make comments on all papers; it's a larger responsibility than you might think, especially when the presenters don't get their papers to you until only a few days prior to the conference!

Endowment for the Humanities speaker series. University of Northern Colorado, Greeley, and El Pueblo Museum, Pueblo.

Invited lecturer, "Telling the Indian Story: New Voices New Questions." New Mexico Endowment for the Humanities Speaker Series, Palace of the Governors, Santa Fe, and University of New Mexico, Albuquerque.

Guest speaker, "Historical Perspectives on Cultural Diversity." NAU's Learning Alliance Interactive teleconference series (via satellite): "The Cultural Diversity Debate and Beyond."

1993: Session presenter: "Ethical Issues in Research with American Indians." "Contemporary Issues in Human Subjects Research: Challenges for Today's Institutional Review Boards" conference, Tempe AZ.

1992: Guest speaker, "After 500 Years: Looking to the Future." Native American Heritage Week, NAU.

Guest speaker, "The Legacy of the Native Americans to the More Recent European Guests." Texas Committee for the Humanities Conference, "Encounter of Two Worlds: Confrontation, Fact, Fiction, And Synthesis," Amarillo TX.

1991: Panelist, "American Indian Women." American Historical Association Annual Conference, session titled "Sex, Race, and the Politics of Conquest," Chicago.

Guest speaker, "American Indians as Monitors of Their Own Education." American Indian Cultural Heritage Celebration, NAU.[48]

Session commentator, "Class, Race, Gender, and Ethnicity." Graduate Interdisciplinary Conference, NAU.

Guest speaker, "Problems of Race and Identity." Arizona Humanities Council's Renaissance World of Christopher Columbus Summer Seminar for Teachers, Flagstaff.

Guest speaker, "The Cherokee Female Seminarians: 'Red' Feminists and Leaders of a Changing Culture." NAU Women's Lecture Series.

---

48. Again, the home institution talks may not be impressive, but young scholars should list all their speaking engagements. It shows that you are active and are becoming experienced at public speaking. It also reflects your desirability, although keep in mind that many search committees aren't impressed. Be sure to balance home talks with engagements out of state, if possible. Some students argue that they cannot afford to travel, but a case can be made that you can't afford not to travel.

1990: Guest speaker: "The Cherokee Female Seminary." Ford Foundation Annual Conference of Fellows, Irvine CA.

Presenter, "Cherokee Male and Female Seminarians in the Twentieth Century." Western History Association Annual Conference, Reno.

Presenter, "Ancestry Sacrificed to Greed: The Desecration of American Indian Culture." Australian and New Zealand American Studies Annual Conference, Sydney.

Presenter, "American Indian Burial Site Desecration Outside the Southwest." NAU Department of History Conference, "Remains and Relics: 'Art' and Human Rights."

Plenary speaker, "The Importance of American Indian Studies in Colleges and Universities." National Endowment for the Humanities Phase III Institute, Tempe AZ.

1989: Session chair for session "American Indian Education," American Society for Ethnohistory Annual Conference, Chicago.

Guest speaker, "Enduring Legacies: The Cherokee Male and Female Seminaries." Northeastern State University's Annual Symposium on the American Indian, Tahlequah OK.

Guest speaker, "American Indians in Indian Territory/Oklahoma." Ft. Worth Genealogical Society Speaker Series.

Presenter, "A Garden of Rose Buds: The Cherokee Female Seminary." Center for Arkansas and Regional Studies Conference, Fayetteville.

1988: Presenter, "Ann Florence Wilson: Matriarch of the Cherokee Female Seminary." Oklahoma Historical Society Annual Conference, Arrowhead Lodge.

Presenter, "An Ounce of Prevention: Health Care at the Cherokee Female Seminary, 1876–1909." Phi Alpha Theta Regional Conference, Waco TX. (Won Phi Alpha Theta writing/research award.)

1985: Presenter, "Indians and Archaeologists: Is There a Middle Ground?" Texas Archaeological Society 56th Annual Meeting, San Antonio.

Presenter, "The Cherokee Female Seminary." Phi Alpha Theta Regional Conference, Wichita Falls TX.

Presenter, "Indians and Museums: The Living and the Dead." Texas Association of Museums' Annual Meeting and Trustee's Conference, Dallas.

SOME BIOGRAPHICAL INFORMATION, INTERVIEWS, ETC.[49]

Abbott, Devon. "'Gentleman' Tom Abbott: Middleweight Champion of the Southwest." *Chronicles of Oklahoma* 68 (spring 1990): 426–37.

Amarillo Borger News Herald, January 5, 1992, p. 3B.

Amarillo Sunday News-Globe, January 5, 1992, p. 5D.

Arizona Daily Sun, March 24, 1993, p. 2.

Arizona Daily Sun, February 25, 1999.

Arizona Daily Sun, October 8, 2000, pp. A1, A11.

Indian Country Today, first week of December 1997.

Ft. Worth Star Telegram, May 20, 1986, pp. A11, A16.

Ft. Worth Star Telegram, May 21, 1986, p. A16.

Ft. Worth Star Telegram, July 20, 1988, p. A5.

"Mihesuah Promotes Native American Empowerment." *NAU Today,* May/June 2003, pp. 3, 7.

Monoghan, Peter. "Challenging the Status Quo in Native American Studies." *Chronicle of Higher Education,* January 17, 2003, http://chronicle.com/weekly/v49/i19/19a01601.htm.

Morgan, Phillip Carroll. "It Is Said: Supernaturalism in the Fiction of Choctaw Authors Louis Owens and Devon A. Mihesuah." Master's thesis, University of Oklahoma, 2001.

Mountain Campus News, January 1990, p. 5.

Mountain Campus News Special Supplement, "Who's Who in Native American Programs at NAU," February 1992.

Mountain Campus News, June–July 1992, p. 3.

Native America Calling, November 29, 2000, http://www.nativecalling.org.

Native America Calling, March 31, 2004.

Navajo-Hopi Observer, July 8, 1992, p. 9.

Navajo Times, December 4, 1997, p. A3.

NPR 90.9 WBUR Boston, *Only a Game,* talk show, March 13, 2004.

The Pine (NAU), fall 1999.

"Promoting Native American Empowerment." *Navajo-Hopi Observer,* April 9, 2003, p. 2.

49. It is a good idea to list each time you are discussed, interviewed, or profiled. Readers need to know that you are "out there" (in more ways than one sometimes), and they can access this information if they want to.

Reference Encyclopedia of the American Indian. New York, 1990, p. 737.
TCU Daily Skiff, December 3, 1987, p. 2.
This Is TCU Magazine, December 1988, pp. 12–14.
Tyler [TX] Morning Telegraph, July 14, 1988, pp. 1, 6.
Who's Who Among America's Teachers. Lake Forest IL: Educational Communications, 1996.

LIST OF REFERENCES[50]

---

50. Some cvs contain a list of references. Do not list anyone's name unless you have his/her permission. There also is no need to list names unless you are applying for a job.

Suggestions for Writing a Book Review

Writing a book review is not the same as writing a book report—you know, those assignments we all did in high school that required us to tell the teacher what the book was about. A book review is not a description. It is a critique, a concise evaluation of a book. Book reviews are crucial aspects of discussing what is happening in the fields of Native Studies and in Native literature. There are many debates and volatile arguments swirling about, and a proper critique of books can help sort out the various points of view.

Most journals have word-length requirements that limit how much you can include. A formula that I have found works well for my students and me is the following:

● Identify your book with a heading:

Donald Worcester. *The Apaches: Eagles of the Southwest*. Norman: University of Oklahoma Press, 1979. Illustrations, maps, graphs, index.

● First paragraph: two or three sentences about the author (where he/she was trained; tribal background if any; previous publications, etc.)

● Two paragraphs: Thesis of the book. Do not give a chapter-by-chapter description. A brief summary of the book is not easy to write, so you may have to rewrite several times.

● Two paragraphs: Your critique of the book. Include its accuracy, author bias (including racism and sexism); its writing style (lively, boring, etc.); who you would recommend read this book; comparison of the book to other works on the subject; strengths and weaknesses; political ramifications of the contents and views; contributions to the field.

● At the end of the review, type your name and under that, add your institution:

Devon A. Mihesuah

Northern Arizona University

Remember that book reviews are written to inform others about a book. The challenge is that you must be thorough yet relatively brief. If the book you are reviewing is important (either good or bad) then ask the editor if you can extend the length.

Sometimes reviewers are asked to review numerous books on the same topic in one review. This is a considerable challenge, since not only must you be skilled at comparing and contrasting all the above components, you also have to give each book equal attention.

Q & A

Q: *I want to write reviews, but how can I get an editor to send me a book?*

A: Approach journal editors at conferences or write to them. Tell them you are interested in books in a certain area and you would like to be considered as a reviewer. Don't be shy! Editors always want good reviewers and if you come through with one competent review, you will be called on again. Then you are on your way to becoming a known writer. Good luck!

Q: *Why are so many book reviews positive and offer little in-depth discussion?*

A: This is indeed one problem with finding adequate reviewers. Many readers are afraid to give critical reviews because they do not want to offend the author of the book. Others are afraid that a negative review will impact their careers unfavorably. This is especially true for graduate students and junior scholars. One thing to keep in mind when you are confronted with a difficult book that needs serious critiquing: The author is a big boy or girl and knows the consequences of writing a book in the first place. If the author knowingly puts forth a flawed book, then unless he/she is naive, he/she will expect some backlash. Strange decisions are made all the time in the world of publishing and bad ones need to be brought to our attention.

Index

book signings, 135
Brown, Jennifer, *Strangers in Blood: Fur Trade Company Families in Indian Country*, 19

Caldecott Medal, 66–67
Calloway, Colin G., *Writing in Indian History, 1985–1990*, 34
Caldwell-Wood, Naomi, *Selective Bibliography and Guide for "I" is Not for Indian*, 67
Campbell, Ben Nighthorse, 28
Carter, Asa, *The Education of Little Tree*, 63
casinos, 24
catalogs, 134–35
chat rooms, 43–44
Cherokee Female and Male Seminaries, 35, 36
"Cherokee Princess Grandmother," 17–18
Cherokees, 11, 23, 25, 28, 29, 32, 66
Chickasaws, 29
childrens books: fiction, 64–65; issues when writing, 65–66; stereotyping in, 3, 8–9, 19
Choctaws, 23, 29, 66, 68
"civilization," 25
Clancy, Tom, 110; *Hunt for Red October*, 119
columns, 54
Comanches, 9, 32
commercial presses, 99
conference papers, 55–56
conferences, meeting publishers at, 102–3, 104
Connell, Evan S., *Son of the Morning Star*, 59
contracts, 127–28
Cook-Lynn, Elizabeth, x; *Anti-Indianism in Modern America: A Voice from Tatekeya's Earth*, 6
copy, 135
copyright, 128
cover letters, 93

credit, giving, 78–79
Creeks (Muscogees), 29
Cross, William, 39
current events writing, 52
curriculum vita (cv), 137–56
Curtis, Charles, 27–28
Custer, George Armstrong, 32, 59, 101

Dances with Wolves (movie), 2, 9
Dawes Rolls, 29
deadlines, 128
Decolonizing Methodologies: Research and Indigenous Peoples (Smith), 6, 61
Deloria, Vine, Jr., 120
diseases, 25
"dissertationeze," 59
Doctrine of Discovery, 19–20
Duncan Weekly Eagle (newspaper), 48–49

editing, 81–86; guides, 42; requesting, assistance, 85–86, 130–31
The Education of Little Tree (Carter), 63
e-mail, 44
enthusiasm for writing, 39–43, 45–46
Erdrich, Louis, 2
ethics in writing, 46–47, 49, 74–80
ethnic fraud, 5
ethnographies, 48–49
ethnohistory, 33

fiction, 129–30; challenges in writing, 62–63, 72–73; repetitious writing in, 64, 71; submitting, to university presses, 123–25; what is needed in, 71–72
first look clause, 129–30
Forbes, Jack, x
Frazier, Ian, *On the Rez*, 12
fullblood, 28

Gobel, Paul, 65

Hanta Yo (Hill), 63, 72

CPSIA information can be obtained
at www.ICGtesting.com
Printed in the USA
FSHW021945050121
77442FS